D0607491

the *Farm to Table* cookbook

the *Farm to Table* cookbook

the art of eating locally

Ivy Manning

Photography by Gregor Torrence

This book is dedicated to the farmers and vendors at farmer's markets everywhere.
They get up early, get dirt under their nails, and stand in the blazing sun
and pouring rain to sell us the fruits of their backbreaking labor.
Blessed are the food growers, for we are always hungry.

Printed in China
Published by Sasquatch Books
Distributed by PGW/Perseus
15 14 13 12 11 10 09 08 9 8 7 6 5 4 3 2 1

Cover photograph: Gregor Torrence
Cover design: Kate Basart/Union Pageworks
Interior design and composition: Kate Basart/Union Pageworks
Interior photographs: Gregor Torrence

Library of Congress Cataloging-in-Publication Data
Manning, Ivy.
The farm to table cookbook : the art of eating locally/Ivy Manning ; photography by Gregor Torrence.
p. cm.
Includes bibliographical references and index.
ISBN-13: 978-1-57061-529-0
ISBN-10: 1-57061-529-2
1. Cookery (Natural foods) 2. Farmer's markets. I. Title.

TX741.M345 2008
641.5'636—dc22

2007045851

Sasquatch Books | 119 South Main Street, Suite 400 | Seattle, WA 98104
206.467.4300 | www.sasquatchbooks.com | custserv@sasquatchbooks.com

CONTENTS

ACKNOWLEDGMENTS

I would like to thank my husband, Gregor. This book would not exist without his immense patience, keen photographic eye, and ability to calm me during my many freak-outs. If we can do a book together in our first year of marriage without ending up in divorce court, just think what the future will bring. . . .

Thanks to my brother, Andy Manning, and members of the chefivy.com newsletter for testing recipes and giving me honest feedback. Thanks also to my grandmother, Helen Zalubowski, who gave me my first wad of pizza dough to play with at age 3. I've been hooked on cooking ever since.

I'd like to express my immense gratitude to the busy chefs who contributed recipes; many didn't know me from Eve, but were happy to share their talent and spread the word about local ingredients and good food. Thanks also to the folks at Sasquatch Books, especially my editor, Gary Luke. He had the vision to see the book within me waiting to be born. Also, thanks to Rachelle Longé for her patience, attention to detail, and long, humorous e-mails.

INTRODUCTION

A revolution is taking place in the way Americans eat. Many of us are turning away from highly processed foods and the chronic diseases that are caused by them. Instead, we're turning to farmer's markets and Community Supported Agriculture (CSA) programs to get fresh, locally grown food for our families. The words *local* and *organic*, seen only in grassroots co-ops a few decades ago, are now common at even the largest supermarkets, thanks to the demand we've created. This transition to locally grown organic foods, whether purchased at a farmer's market or a grocery store chain, will make us healthier as a nation, provide support to local family farms, help save our environment, and rekindle our love affair with good food.

With change, however, comes challenge. The farmer's market experience can be daunting. When we wander through the market, elbow to elbow with other foodies, it's easy for us to be seduced by the gorgeous mounds of greens, the vibrant colors of unknown vegetables, and the aroma of sweet berries. Next thing we know, we've brought home more food than we know what to do with, and some of it may die a lonely death in the vegetable keeper because of lack of inspiration in the kitchen, no matter our good intentions.

So how do we take all that gorgeous food fresh from the farmer's market, CSA box, or natural food store to the dining room table?

This book will help answer that question. Here you'll find a seasonal guide of what's best at the market, from familiar favorites to vegetables you may never have heard of, with great recipes on how to use all of the bounty.

The chapters are grouped by season, which will help you get a feel for an intuitive way of cooking that uses ingredients when they're at their peak. The How to Choose sections will help you get the best vegetable bang for your buck and help you navigate through the seemingly endless variations of ingredients so you can buy with confidence.

I've also included a Meet the Producer section in each chapter. I do this in hopes of introducing you to some of the farmers and food artisans that I've been lucky enough to befriend and be inspired by. By introducing them, I also hope to dispel the notion that all farmers are grumpy old men wearing overalls who face their long days of toil with resignation or bitterness. The passion, education, and youthful exuberance of Michael and Jill Paine, Pat Morford, Barb and Fritz Foulke, and Shari Surkin gives us a glimpse of the new face of farming in America. And despite their enormous challenges, individuals like these are reason to be very optimistic for the future of our food culture.

Recipes are based on my years of cooking and teaching in Portland, Oregon, combined with the knowledge and dedication of some of the Pacific Northwest's best chefs. They are leading the charge toward a closer relationship between the farmers who grow our food and the people who consume it. I urge you to support chefs who are cooking with dedication to local and seasonal ingredients. Their expertise in buying farm fresh produce and meats is a guiding force in forming strong local farming communities, and their talent in the kitchen can inspire you to expand your culinary repertoire at home.

I hope this book will have you eager to cook meals using food grown by good stewards of our land. Some recipes are as simple as wrapping fresh figs with prosciutto and throwing them on the grill; others are sophisticated restaurant-style dishes, like elegant poached duck egg and asparagus salad with truffle oil. Let this book inspire you to shop seasonally, cook simply, and taste the food grown near you.

The Flavor of Farm to Table

Why get out of bed early on a weekend morning or join a CSA harvest-box program when the mega-supermarket is there for you with whatever you want whatever the season? Here are a few reasons to feel good about buying locally.

TASTE. Anyone who's ever savored an heirloom tomato still warm from the sun, or popped a berry into their mouths moments after plucking it, knows that food tastes better when it is in season. A strawberry that travels from a nearby farm directly to a farmer's market can be picked when it is ripe and is more likely bred for its delicious flavor, not for its ability to pack without bruising. Locally grown food doesn't have to be fumigated, refrigerated, and packaged to survive a thousand-mile trip; it arrives to you in a more natural and tastier state.

CONNECTION. Americans have become increasingly isolated; we're a nation of individuals separated by our cars, the music on our headphones, and our cell phones. Coming together over food is one of the best ways to know those around us. Talking face-to-face with the person who grew our food in a market setting is one more step toward interconnectedness.

DIVERSITY IN DIET. Corn, potatoes, carrots, and iceberg lettuce make up the majority of our meager vegetable intake. The USDA recommends eating five to seven servings of vegetables a day: eating a diversity of vegetables is key to preventing disease, according to the National Centers For Disease Control & Prevention. It's much easier to let go of old vegetable habits when there's more than flavorless waxed cucumbers and watery white lettuce available; farmer's markets, CSAs, and grocery stores dedicated to selling locally grown products supply many more choices.

SUPPORTING FAMILY FARMS. According to data collected by Local Harvest, a nonprofit organization that promotes local food systems, only eighteen cents of each dollar spent at the supermarket makes it to the farmer who grew your food. The rest goes to transport, packaging, and marketers. The pressures of agribusiness and cheaper imported food are pushing family farms out of business at an alarming rate. By buying locally from smaller farms, we give farmers a fair price for their product and help their farms survive.

LOCATARIANISM. You might hear folks tossing around the terms *locaterian*, or *locavore* to refer to those who eat only locally produced foods. It may seem like an extreme or utopian fad, but according to the World Watch Organization, ingredients in an average American meal travel between 1,500 to 2,500 miles to reach the table and use seventeen times the petroleum products than if they were locally produced. Choosing to buy local goods makes sense financially, nutritionally, and to some degree, politically.

HUMANELY RAISED LIVESTOCK. I'm sure you've heard something about the abysmal conditions animals raised in factory farms are put through. It's not humane and it's certainly not healthy, as outbreaks of mad cow disease and salmonella have aptly shown. Buying meat directly from the folks who raise the animals allows us to question how the livestock was raised.

Tips for Happy Market Going

To make the most of your visit, consider these recommendations.

GET THERE EARLY FOR THE BEST PRODUCE. Items get picked over and begin to wilt in the heat of the day, so give yourself the freshest selection—stop by in the morning. Also, vendors are usually less harried and more able to answer your questions.

TAKE A STROLL THROUGH THE STALLS BEFORE BUYING. You may discover that broccoli looks better at one vendor or that you want to save some money for the beautiful tomatillos at the last stall.

BRING CASH. Most vendors do business on a cash-only basis; do them a favor and bring small denominations. You may want to raid your change jar and pay in coins.

BRING YOUR OWN BAGS (OR A WAGON IF YOU'RE REALLY HUNGRY). Part of buying locally is saving the environment, so reuse plastic bags or bring a tote.

DON'T BE SHY IF YOU'RE STUMPED. Part of the fun of the farmer's market is meeting the folks who grew your food. They are usually happy to answer your questions and help you decide what to do with the things they grow.

BE KIND TO THE VENDORS. Don't forget that often the folks selling the food grew the food too, and their day probably started many hours earlier and won't end until long after you're gone. If you see a vendor who seems very busy or even quiet, offer to fetch coffee, or simply thank them for the phenomenal sweet peas you bought from them the week before.

VOLUNTEER. Many farmer's markets exist because of volunteers' ardent energy. Join a local market committee to help secure space for the market, plan events, put up tents, advertise, and maintain a Web site. Your specific vocational expertise can help ensure that those with green thumbs will continue to come to your market of choice and sell the fruits of their labor.

BUY ORGANIC WHEN YOU CAN. Beyond all the hard work and challenges of running a small farm, those who grow without pesticides and other chemicals are also challenged by smaller yields. Their food may be more expensive, but it is safer to eat and often tastes better. If we don't create a market for organics, then we won't have that choice in the future.

NIBBLE, TASTE, AND SNIFF. Offer to pay for a taste of a mysterious vegetable; ask if you can have a little leaf or take a deep sniff of a ripe melon. You may discover a new vegetable or fruit you didn't know you loved.

Going One Step Further

If you're already convinced that being more connected to your food source by buying local is the best choice for you, consider joining a CSA, or "farm share" program. Members typically buy a share in a local farm in spring, helping farmers purchase the supplies they need for the upcoming season. In return, the contributor receives a weekly box of fruits and vegetables from the farm. Some farms have a limited season, perhaps June through October; others operate all year long. It's a bit like Christmas every week: you never know what you're going to get. Some even offer supplemental options like free-range chicken, eggs, honey, or a even a neighboring farm's goat cheese as part of their farm share program. CSA farms typically supply information about what to expect in the coming months; some even share recipes. By absorbing some of the financial costs related to sustaining a small farm, you become a positive member of the food chain.

Wintering Over

If you're not fortunate enough to live in a community with a year-round farmer's market, don't give up! Large grocery store chains are beginning to cater to the growing demand for organic and locally produced food. Ask the manager at your local store to carry local products. Read labels. Before you choose an apple that's been shipped from New Zealand, see if there is an apple that's been grown closer to home. If it's January, pass on the mealy pink tomatoes flown in from overseas in favor of a locally grown root vegetable you may never have tried. The occasional banana or mango isn't a bad thing—just be more conscious of the choices you make when buying food.

SPRING

ALL AT ONCE, as if all of nature got together and decided *okay now*, spring arrives. A trip to the farmer's market in early March offers the usual wintry roots and dried goods like nuts and honey, but one vendor will display a pile of crimson rhubarb, a sight that gets die-hard market shoppers a little giddy. It's a sign of promise; if something so vibrant came out of the earth now, in just a few weeks there will be a little more . . . such as the first crisp asparagus and earthy morel mushrooms. A few weeks later fava beans will be in, their leathery pods concealing buttery bites to pair with young sheep's milk cheese and baby artichoke hearts, then sweet English peas to stir into risotto and baby vegetables to decorate lamb stew. Best of all, local strawberries will come at the end of spring, and shoppers won't be able to help themselves from eating a pint while browsing the market. It's a time of leafy green promise, each week revealing delicious new items to make our palates feel alive again.

meet the producer

It's 6 p.m. on a drizzly Saturday in late spring, and Pat Morford's normally bubbly energy seems a bit dampened. "It's been a long day," she explains as she hauls a huge cooler of her farmstead cheeses into Curds and Whey, an indie cheese shop in Portland. Her long, braided gray hair is damp, and she's still wearing the handmade red apron painted with frisky goats that she wore to the farmer's market this morning. "In fact," she says, setting down the cooler and smoothing her hair, "it's been a long couple of weeks."

It's kidding season at the Morfords' ten-acre farm in Logdon, Oregon. Pat has been up night and day helping her does give birth, along with caring for the rest of her seventy-two Alpine goats, keeping on top of orders for her River's Edge Chèvre business, selling at farmer's markets, and delivering to cheese shops, grocery stores, and restaurants. She's been up and running since 5 a.m. and looks nearly beat, but as soon as we sit down to talk about her goats, her eyes suddenly light up.

Pat has been fond of goats since her father brought three to their home on Vashon Island, Washington, when Pat was eight years old. She immediately fell in love with the social creatures and has kept goats on and off ever since. "They become members of our family. We name each one—there's Arial, Ice Cream [who looks like fudge ripple], Biscotti, and Xander. They climb all over me, take hikes with us in the forest . . . they'd live in the house with us if we let them," she says, waving her hand as if to shoo away the thought of a house full of goats.

Her original interest was in breeding dairy goats, for which she's received numerous awards. But with goats comes upkeep and too much milk. "We had to do something value-added to the milk, so we went to cheese. I love the whole artistic aspect of the cheese; there are so many different things you can do with it," she says, nibbling a thin shaving of her newest invention: an earthy washed rind cheese named St. Olga in honor of her mother. The stout beer she brushes on the cheese comes from Siletz Brewing, just a few miles down the road from her farm. "I like to keep things local," she says mirthfully.

Pat makes lovely young chèvres—the tangy spreadables often seen at markets—mixed with pesto, sundried tomatoes, and hazelnuts. But what sets her apart is her ambitious work making European bloomy rind cheeses. Her pyramid-shaped Cape Foulweather, which is rubbed with vegetable ash, boasts a buttery, near-liquid interior when ripe that rivals the imported French soft-ripened cheeses sold in gourmet stores. Her Illahee Tomme is also a Euro-inspired farmstead cheese, made with raw milk, ripened six months, and rubbed with truffle oil. Each cheese is a different expression of artisan cheesemaking, and each year Pat develops new products that look more Parisian *fromagerie* than American Colby.

"Good cheese comes from good milk," Pat explains. "The barnyard flavor of bad cheese comes from the air the animals breathe; fetid air will affect the milk. Our goats have access to the pasture and woods where they graze on hundreds of plants—trefoil, tussock grass, even blackberries. We add a supplement of eastern Oregon alfalfa and a custom grain mix that's made locally. So it's good, clean milk, and it's really good cheese."

Since opening River's Edge Chèvre in 2005, Pat has made a name for herself. Her cheeses are sold as far away as Murray's in New York City (a mecca for farmstead cheese lovers) and appear on cheese lists at fine restaurants up and down the West Coast.

Though Pat can barely keep up with demand, she's not able to support her family with the cheese business alone. Her husband, George, continues his day job in the commercial fishing industry, while Pat works nonstop with just enough help from her two adult daughters and a hired hand. "I wish I could hire more help, but everything is so expensive now—the packaging, the special feed for the goats, gas to deliver the cheese. Customers are paying what I'm asking for [$15 to $36 per pound], but I can't charge more. Our society has gotten too used to not having to pay anything for our food, so much of it is mass-produced and so lacking. Good food is important; it's what nourishes our bodies and teaches our children what it is to eat well," she says ruefully.

Pat plans to expand her operations to sixty milking goats plus a few ewes, but rejects the idea of becoming a large-scale operation. She is adamant about keeping the quality of the cheese high by making it in small batches. "When it gets so large that you get into the industrial part of it, it's not personal anymore. I wouldn't be able to have the attachment with the animals, and then why do it? I love my goats—why else would I work this hard?"

Home-Cured Salmon on Rye with Pickled Onions and Fresh Horseradish Cream

6 to 8 appetizer servings

When wild Pacific Chinook (also called king) salmon comes to farmer's markets (from about April to October), buy a firm piece to cure with salt, sugar, and fresh dill. After 3 or 4 days, the fish becomes rich and sweet, making an easy feast when sliced paper-thin and stacked on artisan bread with pickled onions and fresh horseradish cream. For a more substantial meal, pile thin slices on a bowl of linguini and cream sauce spiked with lemon zest.

FOR THE SALMON:

1 to 2 pounds wild salmon, skin on
¼ cup kosher salt
¼ cup sugar
¼ cup lightly packed brown sugar
Freshly ground black pepper
1 cup chopped fresh dill

FOR THE PICKLED ONIONS:

⅓ cup white vinegar
2 cups water
1 tablespoon kosher salt
1 tablespoon sugar
1 teaspoon coriander seeds
1 bay leaf
2 garlic cloves, peeled and smashed
1 teaspoon black peppercorns
1 medium red onion, thinly sliced

FOR ASSEMBLY:

1 ounce (about 3 tablespoons) fresh horseradish root, peeled and grated, or 2 teaspoons prepared horseradish
½ cup sour cream
2 tablespoons water
½ teaspoon salt
12 slices rye sandwich bread

1. Begin curing the fillets 3 to 4 days before you plan to serve them. Using tweezers, carefully remove and discard any pin bones that run along the center of the fillets. Rinse and pat dry with paper towels.
2. Mix the salt, sugars, and a liberal amount of pepper in a small bowl. Rub the mixture on both sides of the fillets. Press the dill onto the fleshy side and wrap tightly in several layers of plastic wrap. (If you are using one large fillet, cut it in half and stack the halves with the fleshy sides facing each other.) Place the fillets in a large sealable plastic bag and then put it on a dinner plate. Top with another plate and place a few jars on the top plate to weigh it down. Put the fillets in the refrigerator and allow them to cure for 3 to 4 days (no longer than 4 days). Turn the bag over a few times during curing.
3. When you are ready to serve, rinse off the curing mixture and pat the fillets dry with paper towels. Using a sharp, flexible slicing knife held at a 45-degree angle, thinly slice the fillets. Slice only what you will eat immediately; refrigerate the remainder tightly wrapped in fresh plastic wrap for 4 to 5 days.
4. Combine the vinegar, water, salt, sugar, coriander, bay leaf, garlic, and peppercorns in a small, nonreactive saucepan and simmer over medium heat for 10 minutes. Put the onion in a large nonreactive bowl and pour the vinegar mixture over it. Marinate uncovered for 1 hour before serving. Pickled onions can be kept refrigerated in an airtight container for several weeks.
5. Combine the horseradish with the sour cream, water, and salt in a small serving bowl.
6. To serve, cut the bread slices into quarters. Lay generous portions of salmon on each slice and top with pickled onions and horseradish cream.

How to Choose: Horseradish is a root that looks something like a thick, soil-covered white carrot. It is available year-round but is best in colder months. Look for firm roots with no soft spots. You can refrigerate in a dry plastic bag for up to 5 days. Though the raw flesh is eye-wateringly pungent, cooking will transform it into a mellow, buttery vegetable that does well alongside roasts or in stew.

Spicy Minced Pork in Lettuce Bundles

8 appetizer servings

This Thai-inspired dish of minced pork with the fresh flavors of cilantro, mint, and lime in lettuce leaf wrappers is a perfect spring appetizer or cocktail party nibble. Butter lettuce, young romaine leaves, or red leaf lettuce all work great—just put out a bountiful platter of lettuce leaves, let your guests spoon filling into them, and enjoy this taco-style treat.

1 pound pork loin or lean boneless chops
1 tablespoon vegetable oil
2 teaspoons finely chopped garlic
2 green onions, finely chopped
1½ teaspoons minced fresh ginger
1½ teaspoons toasted sesame oil
2 tablespoons soy sauce
1½ teaspoons chili paste or sauce, such as Sriracha
3 tablespoons chopped cilantro leaves
2 tablespoons finely chopped fresh mint
Juice of 1 lime
1 head butter lettuce, washed and leaves separated

1. Trim the fat off the pork. Freeze the meat for 30 minutes or until it is a little firm, which makes it easier to cut. Finely mince the meat with a sharp chef's knife or cleaver.
2. Heat the vegetable oil in a wok over high heat; add the garlic, green onions, and ginger, and stir-fry for 1 minute. Add the pork and continue to stir-fry until it is cooked through, about 3 minutes.
3. Add the sesame oil, soy sauce, and chili paste; continue to cook for 2 minutes, stirring constantly. Transfer the pork mixture to a serving bowl. Gently stir in the cilantro, mint, and lime juice.
4. Decorate a serving plate with the lettuce leaves, splitting the largest leaves to make them more manageable, and serve alongside the pork mixture.

How to Choose: Look for cilantro bunches with fresh green leaves that are relatively free of grit. To clean, swish the cilantro in a large bowl of cold water to remove any clinging dirt. Cilantro will keep for 1 week or more in the refrigerator if you place the bunch upright in a glass filled with a few inches of water and cover it loosely with a plastic bag.

Escarole Caesar Salad

4 servings

Escarole's flat green leaves are often mistaken for a healthy head of Boston lettuce, but the flavor is altogether different. Escarole is from the bitter chicory family and is more closely related to frisée than lettuce. The deep green outer leaves are slightly bitter and are usually cooked like kale or other braising greens. The light green and creamy yellow inner leaves are mild enough to eat raw; their crispness stands up to thick, creamy dressings like the homemade Caesar used here.

FOR THE CROUTONS:

- ½ small loaf (4 ounces) crusty bread
- 2 tablespoons butter
- 1 teaspoon minced garlic
- Salt and freshly ground black pepper

FOR THE SALAD:

- 1 egg yolk
- 1 small (½ teaspoon chopped) garlic clove, green sprout in center removed
- 1 anchovy
- ½ teaspoon Worcestershire sauce
- ½ teaspoon Dijon mustard
- 1 tablespoon fresh lemon juice
- ½ cup extra virgin olive oil
- Salt and freshly ground black pepper
- 1 head (about 12 ounces) escarole
- 1 small block Parmesan cheese, for garnish

1. Preheat the oven to 375°F. Remove the tough bottom crust from the bread and discard; cut the bread into bite-size cubes (you should have 2 heaping cups). Melt the butter in a large sauté pan over medium heat; add the garlic and sauté gently for 30 seconds. Add the bread and toss to coat. Spread the bread on a baking sheet, sprinkle with salt and pepper, and bake, stirring once until golden brown, about 10 minutes. Cool to room temperature.
2. Combine the egg yolk, garlic, anchovy, Worcestershire sauce, mustard, and lemon juice in a blender. With the blender running, hold the lid slightly ajar and add the oil in a very slow, steady stream. Season with salt and pepper to taste.

▸ *continued*

3. Tear off the dark outer leaves from the escarole and reserve for another use. Separate the lighter leaves from their base and tear into bite-size pieces. Swish the leaves in a large bowl of cool water and drain well.
4. Place the escarole and croutons in a large serving bowl and add enough dressing to lightly coat the leaves. Toss well. (Refrigerate the remaining dressing in an airtight container for up to 2 weeks.) With a sharp vegetable peeler, shave thin cheese slices over the salad for garnish.

How to Choose: Look for escarole in winter and spring. If you're using it primarily for salads, choose a compact head with lots of crisp, light-colored leaves. Do not wash before storing; wrap loosely in paper towels and place in a plastic bag in the vegetable keeper. Use within 5 days of purchase, washing well to remove clinging dirt.

Baby Artichoke and Fava Bean Salad with Pecorino

4 side dish servings

Fava beans are paired with baby artichokes for a special-occasion salad or side dish in this recipe. Preparing baby artichokes is a bit easier than more mature artichokes since there's no fuzzy choke in the center to wrestle with. Fava beans are a bit more work: shell them, then blanch the beans and peel away their pastel green leathery skins. Your reward is sweet, buttery beans best served barely cooked with minimal additions like light olive oil or young sheep's milk cheese.

3 pounds young fava beans
Ice water for blanching
1 large lemon, halved
10 baby artichokes
3 tablespoons olive oil
2/3 cup thinly sliced shallots
1/2 cup dry white wine or vermouth
1/2 teaspoon chopped fresh thyme leaves
1/2 cup water or chicken stock
Salt and freshly ground black pepper
2 ounces pecorino or other mild sheep's milk cheese
1 small loaf crusty bread

1. Bring a small pot of water to a boil. Meanwhile, shell the fava beans by snapping off the tip of each pod and pressing at the seam to open the pods. Pop out the beans with your thumb. When the water boils, cook them until they are just tender to the bite, 30 seconds to 1 minute depending on size. Drain and place in the ice water to stop them from overcooking. Peel the tough light green skin from each bean and discard.
2. To prepare the artichokes, fill a medium bowl with cold water and the juice from 1 lemon half. Snap off the leaves until you reach the tender yellow-green core, rubbing all cut surfaces with the remaining lemon half as you work to prevent browning. Slice off the top quarter and then, with a sharp peeler or paring knife, pare away the tough stem and green layer around the base. Halve the artichokes lengthwise and toss them into the lemon water.
3. Heat the oil in a large sauté pan over medium heat, add the shallots, and cook until translucent but not brown, about 4 minutes. Drain the artichokes and pat them dry with paper towels. Add them to the shallots and cook for 10 minutes, stirring occasionally.

continued

4. Raise the heat to medium-high, add the wine, and boil until the wine is reduced by half, about 8 minutes. Add the thyme and water, cover, and simmer for 5 minutes, or until the artichokes are tender when pierced with a fork.
5. Add the fava beans and cook until the beans are just warm, about 1 minute. Season with salt and pepper and transfer the mixture to a serving dish. With a sharp vegetable peeler, shave the cheese over the dish. Serve with the bread as a first course or as a side dish for chicken or fish.

How to Choose: Fava beans come encased in large, thick green pods 4 to 7 inches long. Choose pods that are vibrantly green (a few black specks are normal). Avoid beans that have soft brown spots, which is a sign of age. The beans, once shelled, have a leathery, light green skin encasing them. This skin is edible only when the beans are very young. Taste one to decide whether you'll need to blanch and peel them. Three pounds of fava beans will yield about one pound of peeled, ready-to-eat beans. Within a few days of purchase, peel and freeze the beans you don't use.

Shaved Fennel, Cannellini Bean, and Tuna Salad

6 servings

Fennel has a fresh, anise-like flavor and crisp texture that lends itself well to salads. This recipe is a great "go-to" recipe when you need a substantial salad to serve at picnics and potlucks.

Some farmers have begun to sell their own dried heirloom shelling beans like Zolfino and Tarbais at farmer's markets; in this recipe their distinct flavor and firm texture make them a great alternative to conventional dried cannellini beans.

1 cup dried cannellini or other dried shelling beans
7 cups cold water
1 bay leaf
2 teaspoons salt
1 garlic clove, peeled
1 small (4 to 6 ounces) fennel bulb
½ cup thinly sliced red onion
One 6-ounce can tuna in oil, undrained
1 tablespoon extra virgin olive oil
Juice of 1 lemon
1 tablespoon apple cider vinegar
¼ cup Italian parsley, finely chopped
Salt and freshly ground black pepper

1. Soak the beans in cool water for at least 8 hours, or overnight. Drain the beans, rinse well, and put in a large saucepan. Add the water, bay leaf, salt, and garlic; bring to a boil. Simmer until the beans are tender, tasting frequently to determine doneness. Cannellini beans take about 40 minutes; other heirloom varieties will take less time, depending on their size and age. Drain the beans and refrigerate until cool.
2. Halve the fennel lengthwise, separate the feathery green fronds from the stalks, and finely chop the fronds. Slice the fennel stalks and bulb as thinly as possible (a mandoline works best).
3. In a large bowl, combine the beans, fennel, onion, tuna and its oil, olive oil, lemon juice, vinegar, and parsley. Toss together gently; add salt and pepper to taste before serving.

How to Choose: Fennel bulbs should have feathery green leaves still attached to assure freshness. Don't buy fennel that has soggy dark leaves. The bulb end should be firm, plump, and pearly white, with no cracks or shriveled bits. Refrigerate, loosely wrapped in plastic, for up to 5 days.

Warm Asparagus with Morels and Poached Duck Egg

4 servings

Pascal Sauton, chef-owner of Carafe in downtown Portland, makes this dish with the first young asparagus of the season. Duck eggs are crucial to this dish, says Chef Sauton. "They are so much richer, the yolk spreads out on the asparagus when you cut it open with your fork, it's *so* good; you can't get that richness with a little chicken egg." Duck eggs are available at farmer's markets and some natural food stores.

2 tablespoons sherry vinegar
6 tablespoons walnut oil (see Resources)
1 teaspoon truffle oil (see Resources)
Fleur de sel (see Resources)
Freshly ground black pepper
2 pounds asparagus
Ice water for blanching
1 cup fresh morel mushrooms
1 cup vegetable stock
2 tablespoons white wine vinegar
4 duck eggs
1 tablespoon finely minced chives

1. Preheat the oven to 200°F. To make the vinaigrette, in a small bowl, whisk the sherry vinegar and oils. Season with Fleur de sel and pepper; set aside.
2. Bring a large pot of salted water to a boil. Bend each asparagus stalk until it snaps, separating the tender part from the woody base; discard the base. Cook the asparagus in the boiling water until its color is bright and it is still crunchy, 1 to 3 minutes depending on the size of the stalks. Drain and blanch immediately in the ice water, and then remove and pat dry with paper towels. Divide the spears among 4 plates.
3. Rinse the mushrooms in several changes of cold water, drain, and trim the stem bottoms. In a small saucepan, bring the stock to a simmer and then poach the mushrooms gently until tender, 5 to 8 minutes. Remove them with a slotted spoon and divide among the asparagus. Place the asparagus plates in a warm oven while you poach the eggs.

▸ *continued*

4. Bring 2 quarts of water to a boil in a wide, low saucepan. Reduce the heat to maintain a very low simmer; stir in the wine vinegar. Crack 1 egg into a small teacup; gently slip the egg into the water. Poach eggs, two at a time, for 3½ to 4 minutes; the whites should be firm, the yolks still liquid. Remove from pan with a slotted spoon and set aside. Repeat with the remaining eggs.
5. Remove eggs from the water with a slotted spoon and place one on each asparagus plate. Sprinkle with the vinaigrette, chives, Fleur de sel, and pepper, and serve immediately.

How to Choose: Asparagus comes in a range of sizes and colors, from thick white stalks, which have been hooded to prevent chlorophyll from forming, to rangy green spears thinner than a pencil. One type is not necessarily better than another; it's all a matter of preference. With all asparagus, look for tightly formed tips and plump stalks. Avoid bunches that have mushy ends, wrinkled stalks, or tips beginning to open. Keep asparagus in a plastic bag with the base of the stalks wrapped in moist paper towels; store in the vegetable keeper for up to 3 days.

Kohlrabi Salad with Pea Shoots

6 servings

Ah, the poor maligned kohlrabi. When I was doing research for this book, I asked folks who were members of CSA programs the vegetable they wished they'd never see in their weekly box again, and most answered "kohlrabi." Truthfully, I didn't think I cared for it either until I tried this truly awesome recipe from Chef Fearn Smith of The Farm Café in Portland. Kohlrabi is a member of the odiferous brassica family (a cousin of cabbage), but it has a rather benign flavor, something like a cross between green cabbage and broccoli, yet milder and crisper. This recipe should change your mind if you ever thought of kohlrabi as an "ick" vegetable.

2 large red or green kohlrabi bulbs
1 large carrot, peeled
1 teaspoon fennel seeds
2 tablespoons rice wine vinegar
½ teaspoon kosher salt
½ teaspoon freshly ground black pepper
2 tablespoons olive oil
1 teaspoon toasted sesame oil
2 cups pea shoots (optional)

1. With a sharp chef's knife, cut the tough outer skin and stems from the kohlrabi. Julienne the kohlrabi with a mandoline or sharp knife (you will have about 4 cups), and then julienne the carrots.
2. Toast the fennel seeds in a small dry sauté pan over medium heat until they begin to brown slightly and smell toasty. Transfer them to a mortar and pestle or clean spice grinder and grind into a coarse powder.
3. Combine the fennel powder, vinegar, salt, and pepper in a small bowl. Slowly whisk in the oils. Pour over the vegetables and toss to coat.
4. Chop the pea shoots into 1-inch pieces and toss into the salad immediately before serving.

How to Choose: Kohlrabi is available almost year-round, but you'll find it most often in late spring to early summer. Small to medium kohlrabi (no bigger than a fist) have the mildest flavor. If possible, buy it with the leaves still attached; they're an indicator of freshness. If the leaves are yellow or are wilting, don't buy it. The leaves have a delicious, satisfying texture when boiled and lightly dressed (see recipe, page 18).

A Versatile Recipe for the Hearty Greens You Don't Know What to Do With

2 to 4 servings

Just about every visit to the farmer's market or delivery from a CSA will yield one big, bushy bunch of greens. I suspect that too often these gorgeous greens are just discarded. Whether attached to beets, kohlrabi, turnips, or just simple kale, those coarse-looking greens are indeed edible, and I don't mean in that bland macrobiotic-steamed-brown-rice kind of way. They are really yummy, especially prepared in this simple Japanese-inspired style. There are no quantities here; each batch of greens will have a different flavor and quantity; just sprinkle the other ingredients sparingly on the greens until you get a flavorful blend.

1 bunch hearty greens—kohlrabi, beets, turnips, or kale
Toasted sesame oil
Good-quality soy sauce
*Furikake** or toasted sesame seeds

1. Tear the leaves from their tough ribs and stems. Bring a pot of water to a boil, add the leaves, and boil until tender, 1 to 3 minutes depending on the type of greens.
2. Drain the greens in a colander and push on them to remove as much water as possible.
3. Roughly chop the cooked greens and place them on a serving plate. Sprinkle lightly with sesame oil and soy sauce; toss to coat. Sprinkle with the furikake and serve as a side dish or salad.

* Furikake is a Japanese condiment made from sesame seeds, nori seaweed, and sea salt; it is used as a seasoning for rice and salads. It is available at most Asian grocery stores. You can substitute toasted sesame seeds and a sprinkle of sea salt.

Spring Greens Primer

After four months or more of root vegetables, it's only natural that we crave green and leafy things. Don't fall into the bag-o-supermarket-baby-greens rut—there's a wide range of green edibles to experiment with at your local farmer's market. Though some of the greens listed here are available year-round thanks to their hardiness or hydroponic adaptability, their leaves tend to be more tender and succulent in spring and summer.

1. **CHARD (ALSO CALLED SWISS CHARD):** Use this leafy green from the beet family as you would spinach—younger leaves in salads, older leaves sautéed. The celery-like stems have a beet-like earthiness and are best chopped and cooked separately. Chard ranges from white-stemmed to crimson- and ruby-stemmed varieties; there's little difference among them in flavor. Bright Lights Chard is an attractive variation sold in mixed color bundles with striking yellow, pink, and red stems.

2. **ARUGULA:** The peppery bite of arugula is familiar to most thanks to its role in mesclun green mixes. As the plant ages, the flavor becomes more pronounced and the leaves and stems thicken. Italians use arugula tossed in pastas, on pizzas, and in warm salads. Arugula marries well with creamy goat cheese, lemon, Parmesan cheese, and the flavor of rare grilled beef.

3. **PEA SHOOTS:** These young tendrils of sweet peas are often sold in bulk in a large green tangle. They add a crispy, sweet addition to salads, and as a garnish they make any entrée look like it came from a fancy restaurant. Laotian and Thai cooks stir-fry them for a nanosecond and serve them with rice and a splash of fish sauce. Pea shoots have a short life when harvested; store in a plastic bag in the vegetable keeper and use within a few days of purchase.

4. **DANDELION GREENS:** Familiar to most people as a lawn weed, saw-toothed dandelions (Latin for "lion's teeth") are cultivated and sold in big bunches at markets. These dandelion greens tend to be less astringent than the weeds in your yard. Use the small leaves for salads and save the larger leaves for sautés (the tough stems often need to be removed). Their flavor works especially well with lemon, garlic, and rich creamy cheeses with assertive flavor.

5. **BUTTER LETTUCE:** This sweet, tender lettuce is most commonly sold as Boston and Bibb lettuce. However, Boston lettuce leaves are set wider apart and tend to be a lighter green than the smaller, more flavorful Bibb type. The leaves have a buttery tenderness that pairs well with buttermilk-based dressings, and their shape makes them ideal for wraps with zesty fillings like spicy ground pork or chicken. Store the unwashed heads for a short time; the delicate leaves loose their perkiness quickly.

6. **WATERCRESS:** The small, succulent leaves of this plant have been prescribed over the years for everything from hangovers to liver ailments. The rounded, deep green leaves have a peppery bite that lends a punch to salads, stir fries, and creamy soups. Watercress is sometimes sold with the roots still attached; these bunches can be kept alive in the refrigerator with the roots set in water. You can also plant the roots after you consume the leaves to grow your own watercress. Watercress does well paired with orange or fennel, and in creamy soups.

7. **ESCAROLE (ALSO CALLED FLAT-LEAF CHICORY OR BATAVIAN ENDIVE):** This light green ruffled head of leaves from the chicory clan is sometimes mistaken for Boston and Bibb lettuce. The leaves tend to be more crisp than lettuce, with a bit of bitterness that's characteristic of chicories. The sturdier outer leaves are good lightly sautéed like lacinato kale; the tender inner leaves make a nice addition to salads.

Swiss Chard and Feta Phyllo Pockets with Yogurt Dill Dip

6 servings

This recipe combines tender Swiss chard leaves with spinach and locally made feta cheese for a tasty take on the Greek *spanikopitta* phyllo pies. The goat's milk and sheep's milk feta cheeses offered by cheese makers at farmer's markets are usually a much higher quality than the salty, mass-produced fetas sold in grocery stores. I use the mild, creamy goat's milk feta from Alsea Acres, available at Portland-area farmer's markets and online (see Resources). Use the best feta you can find.

FOR THE PHYLLO POCKETS:

- 1/3 cup white rice
- 2/3 cup cold water, plus additional as needed
- 1 bunch (1 pound) fresh spinach
- 2 bunches (2 pounds) Swiss chard, washed well and dried
- 1/3 cup plus 2 tablespoons olive oil, divided
- 1 leek cut lengthwise, white and light green parts sliced into thin rings
- 1 teaspoon minced garlic
- 7 ounces (about 1 1/2 cups) feta cheese
- 1/3 cup fresh dill, chopped
- 3 tablespoons grated Parmesan cheese
- 1/2 teaspoon ground nutmeg
- 2 eggs
- Salt and freshly ground black pepper
- 1/2 pound phyllo dough, thawed
- 1/3 cup butter, melted, plus additional for brushing

FOR THE YOGURT DIP:

- 2 cups plain full-fat yogurt
- 2 tablespoons chopped fresh dill
- 1 small garlic clove, mashed to a paste
- Salt and freshly ground black pepper

1. Combine the rice and water in a small saucepan and bring to a boil over high heat. Cover, reduce the heat, and simmer until tender, about 15 minutes. Pour the rice into a large bowl and refrigerate until cool.

▸ *continued*

2. Cut off the stems from the spinach and discard. Place the leaves in a large bowl of cold water and swirl; the grit will sink to the bottom. Scoop out the leaves, change the water, and repeat. Scoop the leaves into a salad spinner or colander and dry well.
3. Separate the tough chard stalks from the leaves, finely chop the stalks, and tear the leaves into bite-size pieces. Heat 2 tablespoons of the oil in a large sauté pan or wok over medium-high heat. Add the chard stalks and leek; cook until the leek has softened, about 5 minutes. Add the garlic and cook for 1 minute.
4. Reduce the heat to medium, add the chard leaves, and toss with tongs to coat the leaves with oil. Cook for 3 minutes; add the spinach one handful at a time until all the leaves are added.
5. Transfer the mixture to a fine-mesh sieve or colander and press with a spatula to extract as much moisture as possible. Mix the greens with the rice and refrigerate for 10 minutes. Stir in the feta, dill, Parmesan, nutmeg, and eggs. Season with salt and pepper. Preheat the oven to 350°F.
6. Stack 2 sheets of phyllo dough on a cutting board with the long side facing you. Cover the remaining dough with a clean dish towel to keep it from drying out.
7. Combine the butter and remaining oil in a measuring cup. Pick up the right half of the top phyllo sheet, as if turning the page of a book. Lightly brush the bottom sheet with the butter-oil mixture, lower the top sheet onto the buttered sheet, and press to seal the right side of the sheets together. Repeat with the left side. Cut the dough into four 3½-inch-wide vertical strips.
8. Place a heaping tablespoon of the filling on the bottom left corner of one strip. Fold the bottom edge upward, lining it up with the edge on the right side to make a triangular pocket. Fold the pocket upward, then to the left and so on as if folding a flag. Repeat with the remaining strips.
9. Place the pockets on a cookie sheet and brush lightly with butter. Repeat with the remaining dough and filling. (The pockets may be prepared ahead at this point and frozen on cookie sheets until solid. Transfer to a sealable plastic bag and use within 3 months. To bake, defrost the pockets at room temperature for 1 hour and bake as directed.) Bake the pockets until they are golden brown, 40 minutes.
10. To make the dip, whisk the yogurt, dill, garlic, and salt and pepper to taste. Serve alongside the hot phyllo pockets.

Fresh Pea and Pancetta Risotto

4 main course servings

This dish, called *risi e bisi* in the Veneto region of Italy, is made with freshly shelled peas, Arborio rice, and pancetta (Italian salt-cured bacon) to celebrate the season's sweetest peas. The simplicity of the dish demands that you use the freshest peas and mild homemade chicken stock for best results. If you can't find pancetta, use locally made nitrate-free bacon that hasn't been heavily smoked.

1 pound (1 cup shelled) fresh English peas
7 cups homemade chicken stock
2 tablespoons olive oil
½ cup (2 ounces) finely chopped pancetta
1 cup finely chopped onion
1½ cups Arborio or Vialone Nano rice
½ cup dry white wine
1 cup grated Parmesan cheese
¼ cup minced Italian parsley
Salt and freshly ground black pepper

1. Shell the peas and set aside. Bring the stock to a low simmer in a large stockpot.
2. Heat the oil in a medium saucepan over medium-high heat. Add the pancetta and sauté until it has rendered its fat, about 4 minutes. Add the onion and continue to cook until the onion is tender and the pancetta just begins to brown, about 6 minutes.
3. Add the rice and cook, stirring constantly, for 1 minute, or until the rice is lightly toasted. Add the wine and cook, stirring constantly, until the wine is absorbed. Add one ladle (about 8 ounces) of stock and bring to a simmer, stirring constantly until the liquid is absorbed. Continue adding stock in intervals until almost all the stock is used, about 15 minutes.

continued

4. Reduce the heat to medium, add half the peas and the remaining stock, and cook for 3 minutes. Bite into a grain of rice; if it has an opaque white center the diameter of a pin and has just a hint of chew, it is perfectly cooked. The mixture will be slightly soupy, the traditional consistency of risi e bisi.
5. Remove the saucepan from the heat; stir in the remaining peas, cheese, and parsley. Season with salt and pepper and serve.

How to Choose: English peas, sometimes called shelling peas, are sweetest right off the vine. Just like corn, their sugars start to convert to starch the moment they are picked, so it's worth asking how old the peas are before buying. Better yet, ask for a sample. Look for vibrantly green pods with bulging peas inside. Peas that are crowded in the pod and have taken on a square shape have been on the vine too long and will be starchy, not sweet. Refrigerate peas wrapped loosely in a plastic bag for no longer than 1 day, or shell and freeze them immediately after purchase.

Asparagus and Caramelized Leek Bread Pudding

6 to 8 servings

This savory bread pudding is a good option as either a brunch entrée or a side dish for grilled chicken or fish. Use thick asparagus to make sure it won't overcook while baking. Lemon thyme, a hearty variety of thyme with green and yellow variegated leaves, gives the bread pudding a refreshing lemon flavor. Regular fresh thyme can be substituted.

10 ounces (about 7 cups) focaccia or French bread, cut into 1-inch cubes
1 pound asparagus, tough ends snapped off
Ice water for blanching
1 medium leek
4 teaspoons olive oil
4 cups half-and-half
8 eggs
Zest of 1 lemon
1 teaspoon chopped fresh lemon thyme
½ cup grated Parmesan cheese
½ cup grated Pecorino Romano cheese

1. Spread the bread cubes on a baking sheet and let stand overnight to become stale, or quick-dry in a 200°F oven for 40 minutes.
2. Preheat the oven to 350°F and butter a 13- by 9- by 2-inch baking dish. Bring a large pot of water to a boil, add the asparagus, and cook until it is bright green, about 2 minutes. Drain and blanch immediately in the ice water; remove and set aside.
3. Remove the dark green part of the leek and discard. Halve the leek lengthwise, rinse well between layers, and thinly slice. In a sauté pan, heat the oil over medium heat. Add the leeks and sauté until they begin to brown, about 10 minutes. Add a few tablespoons of water and continue to cook for 5 minutes, or until the leeks are caramel colored and tender; set aside.
4. In a medium bowl, whisk the half-and-half, eggs, lemon zest, and thyme. Put the bread cubes in the prepared baking dish and sprinkle on the leeks. Arrange the asparagus on top and pour the egg mixture over all. Press with a spatula to submerge the bread cubes; sprinkle the top with the cheeses.
5. Cover the dish loosely with foil and bake until the edges are golden brown and a butter knife inserted into the center comes out clean, about 1 hour and 15 minutes. Cool for 20 minutes, cut into squares, and serve.

Watercress, Snow Pea, and Shiitake Stir-Fry

4 side dish servings, 2 main course servings with rice

Watercress is an antioxidant-rich superfood, and it's not only good for you, it is incredibly tasty and versatile too. It's a great peppery green when served raw in salads or on tea sandwiches with cream cheese, and it mellows nicely when cooked in soups or stir-frys like the orange-garlic flavored one here.

2 teaspoons cornstarch
2 tablespoons sherry or rice cooking wine
¼ cup fresh orange juice
2 teaspoons brown sugar
2 tablespoons soy sauce
1 teaspoon toasted sesame oil
2 tablespoons vegetable oil
1 tablespoon minced ginger
1 tablespoon minced garlic
2 ounces shiitake mushrooms, stemmed and thinly sliced
4 ounces snow peas, strings removed
1 large bunch (about 4 ounces) watercress, roots and tough stems discarded

1. Combine the cornstarch and sherry in a medium bowl; whisk with a fork to dissolve any lumps. Stir in the orange juice, brown sugar, soy sauce, and sesame oil; set aside.
2. Heat the vegetable oil over medium-high heat in a wok or large sauté pan. Add the ginger and garlic and cook for 20 seconds, stirring constantly. Add the mushrooms and cook until they begin to turn golden brown, about 3 minutes.
3. Add the snow peas and cornstarch mixture to the pan and cook until the sauce is thick and bubbly, about 2 minutes. Remove from the heat and add the watercress, tossing until it has wilted slightly. Serve immediately.

How to Choose: Watercress should be as fresh as possible—it is often sold with the roots still attached. Pick bunches that have no yellowing or slimy leaves. To store, remove the tie that holds the bunch together, place in a jar with a bit of water, cover loosely with a plastic bag, and refrigerate. Use within a few days of purchase. Plant the root bundle and stems if they are fairly healthy; you may be able to continue to grow your own watercress leaves.

Tortellini in Creamy Tarragon Sauce with Fresh Peas and Ham

4 servings

While visiting Verona, Italy, I had a magical meal of plump tortellini, sweet peas, and prosciutto in a light cream sauce. The name of the dish, *Tortellini alla Medici*, was memorable because the prominent Medici family of Florence had funded many of the Renaissance artists I was in Italy to study. This creamy pasta dish is most likely named after the Medicis because it's as rich and opulent as they were. I use fresh, locally made cheese tortellini sold at my farmer's market. Use the best quality tortellini or ravioli you can find.

1 tablespoon olive oil
2 tablespoons finely chopped shallots
⅓ cup dry vermouth or dry white wine
4 ounces ham, rind removed and julienned
2 tablespoons fresh tarragon leaves, stemmed and finely chopped
2 cups heavy cream
1 pound fresh cheese tortellini
1 cup fresh English peas, shelled
Salt and freshly ground black pepper
½ cup grated Parmesan cheese

1. Heat the olive oil in a large sauté pan over medium-high heat; add the shallots and sauté until softened, about 3 minutes. Add the vermouth and simmer until almost all the liquid is gone. Add the ham, tarragon, and cream; bring to a gentle simmer over medium heat until thickened slightly, about 10 minutes.
2. Meanwhile, bring a large pot of salted water to a boil. Add the tortellini and reduce the heat to maintain a simmer (do not cook in rapidly boiling water or the pasta may burst open). Cook until tender, 3 to 7 minutes, depending on the size and thickness of the pasta.
3. Drain the tortellini and transfer to the cream sauce; stir in the peas and cook for 1 minute. Season with salt and pepper, sprinkle with the Parmesan, and serve.

Spinach and Roasted Shallot Flan

6 servings

Renee Erickson, co-owner and chef of Seattle's Boat Street Cafe, makes this savory flan all year using whatever is in season. "The basic recipe is really simple. You can use other vegetable combinations like cherry tomato, tarragon, and chèvre in summer or wild mushrooms, thyme, and Gruyère in fall; almost anything works," she advises. Serve this crustless quiche with a simple green salad and a baguette for a vegetarian meal or as a side dish for roast chicken.

4 medium (4 ounces) shallots
1 tablespoon olive oil
Salt and freshly ground black pepper
½ bunch (2 cups loosely packed leaves) spinach
2 tablespoons fresh marjoram leaves, or ½ teaspoon dried marjoram
3 eggs
1½ cups heavy cream
¼ teaspoon Dijon mustard
1 pinch freshly grated nutmeg
½ cup grated Parmesan cheese
2 ounces white cheddar cheese, thinly sliced

1. Preheat the oven to 400°F. Peel the shallots and trim off the roots while leaving the root end intact so the shallots don't break apart during cooking. Halve them lengthwise. Heat the oil in a small ovenproof sauté pan over medium-high heat; add the shallots and sauté until they begin to brown, about 2 minutes. Using tongs, carefully turn them over, season with salt and pepper, and transfer the pan to the oven. Bake until they are soft and caramelized, about 30 minutes.

2. Divide the spinach leaves, shallots, and marjoram leaves among 6 custard cups or brûlée dishes, and put them on a baking sheet. Whisk the eggs, cream, mustard, nutmeg, Parmesan, and ½ teaspoon of salt in a medium bowl. Add the mixture to within ½ inch from the top of each custard cup. Sprinkle the white cheddar on top of each, leaving some space around the edges to allow the flan to puff up slightly.
3. Carefully transfer the baking sheet to the oven; bake until the flans are puffy and the custard is just set, about 30 minutes. Cool for 10 minutes before serving.

How to Choose: Look for spinach with small, tender, deep green leaves with no sign of yellowing or wilting. Spinach is grown in sandy soil, so wash it thoroughly. Slice off the stems, remove the twist ties, and dunk the leaves into a large bowl of cold water. Gently swirl to rinse then scoop the leaves out of the water. Repeat the process twice in fresh water and spin the leaves dry in a salad spinner or pat dry with a clean dish towel. Washed and dried spinach can be stored in the vegetable keeper in a bowl topped with a few paper towels for up to 3 days. Do not store in plastic bags; moisture will cause the leaves to deteriorate quickly.

Seared Scallops with Creamed Ramps and Black Truffle

4 servings as an appetizer or light entrée

Ramps, also called wild onions or wild leeks, are a native of North America and belong to the lily family. Available from March to May, they are sold at farmer's markets by the same folks who specialize in other foraged items like wild mushrooms and truffles. They may look like green onions, with a thin white bulb and green leaves, but ramps have broader leaves and a pungent garlic aroma. Chef Jason Wilson of Crush in Seattle cooks ramps in cream to mellow their flavor, pairing them here with sweet seared scallops and a punchy citrus vinaigrette. Use roughly chopped green onions or leeks if ramps are unavailable.

2 tablespoons blood-orange juice
1 tablespoon lime juice
1 tablespoon plus 1 teaspoon lemon juice, divided
1 tablespoon finely chopped parsley
2 teaspoons chopped fresh tarragon
2 teaspoons Dijon mustard
Salt and freshly ground black pepper
¼ cup extra virgin olive oil
1 large bunch (about 8 ounces) ramps
½ cup heavy cream
¼ cup chicken stock
1 bay leaf
1 teaspoon lemon thyme leaves, chopped
1 teaspoon black truffle oil
12 large sea scallops
2 tablespoons vegetable oil
1 black truffle, wiped clean with a damp paper towel

1. Whisk the orange juice, lime juice, 1 tablespoon of the lemon juice, parsley, tarragon, mustard, and ¼ teaspoon each salt and pepper in a medium bowl. Slowly whisk in the olive oil and set aside.

▸ *continued*

2. Wash the ramps thoroughly, peeling off the first layer of the bulb if necessary to remove dirt. Trim off the roots but keep the ramps whole. Combine the cream, remaining lemon juice, stock, and bay leaf in a saucepan; bring to a simmer over medium-high heat and cook for 3 minutes. Add the ramps and cook for 5 minutes, turning them occasionally with tongs. Add the thyme and cook for 2 minutes. Season with salt, pepper, and truffle oil; keep warm over very low heat.
3. Season the scallops generously with salt and pepper. Turn on the kitchen exhaust fan or open a window; searing will cause the room to get smoky. Put the vegetable oil in a large, heavy sauté pan or cast iron skillet and place over high heat. When the oil begins to smoke, carefully add the scallops; reduce the heat to low and sear on one side until golden, about 2 minutes. Turn with tongs and cook for 2 more minutes, or until done to your preference. Meanwhile, warm 4 dinner plates.
4. Divide the ramps and scallops among the plates. Drizzle the perimeters of the plates with a few tablespoons of the citrus vinaigrette mixture. Shave the truffle over each plate with a sharp vegetable peeler and serve.

How to Choose: Look for ramps that still have their roots intact and have fresh-looking green leaves. Pass on bunches with mushy leaves; ramps disintegrate quickly when they are packed together haphazardly. Store ramps wrapped in paper towels and placed in a heavy-duty airtight freezer bag in the vegetable keeper for up to 4 days. The garlicky aroma of the ramps can permeate the refrigerator if stored incorrectly.

Halibut Cheeks with Morel Mushrooms

4 servings

Halibut cheeks are a delicacy, with a meaty, scallop-like texture and a sweet flavor. Find them at grocery stores and fish shops, or use thin slices of halibut instead. And just as halibut comes into season on the West Coast, morels begin to appear at farmer's markets. Happily, they have a natural flavor affinity for each other, as amply displayed in Chef Pascal Sauton's recipe here. He serves this dish at Carafe with flour-based gnocchi, but steamed new potatoes are a nice accompaniment too.

¼ cup (½ stick) unsalted butter
1 pound halibut cheeks
Salt and freshly ground black pepper
1 cup all-purpose flour
½ cup thinly sliced shallots
½ cup dry vermouth or dry white wine
2 cups Quick Fish Stock (see recipe, page 36)
20 morel mushrooms, well washed
½ cup crème fraîche
2 pinches Espelette pepper (see *, page 136) or cayenne pepper

1. To clarify the butter, melt it in a glass measuring cup. Allow it to sit for a few minutes, then skim off the white foam that rises to the top. Carefully spoon out the golden liquid into a large sauté pan; discard the milky liquid at the bottom of the cup.
2. Season the halibut with salt and pepper, and lightly dredge it in flour, shaking off the excess. Heat the butter over medium-high heat, add the halibut, and cook until it's golden brown on one side, about 3 minutes. Using tongs, turn it over and continue to cook until it is cooked through, about 3 more minutes. Place it on a dinner plate; loosely wrap the plate with foil.
3. Add the shallots to the pan and sauté until they just begin to brown. Deglaze the pan with the vermouth; simmer until the wine is almost dry. Add the stock and morels, and boil until the stock is reduced by half, about 5 minutes.
4. Reduce the heat to low, stir in the crème fraîche and Espelette pepper, and cook until heated through, about 2 minutes. Add the halibut to the sauté pan to rewarm it. Place the halibut and sauce on a large platter and serve.

How to Choose: Morel mushrooms that look sodden will taste sodden. Look for specimens that are plump but not wet with a relatively small amount of stem. Rinse in several changes of cool water; use a soft baby toothbrush to knock free dirt still clinging to the cap.

Quick Fish Stock

7 cups

Good fish stock can be hard to find, but it is very easy to make. Ask your fishmonger for fish bones—it's a good idea to call ahead so they are set aside for you. Use only bones from mild-flavored fish like halibut, snapper, and trout. Forget the salmon, mackerel, and tuna bones; they're too fishy tasting. Leftover stock freezes well in a sealable freezer bag for up to 3 months.

1 tablespoon vegetable oil
½ cup roughly chopped onion
½ small leek, roughly chopped
½ small fennel bulb, roughly chopped
1 garlic clove
2 pounds fish bones, heads, and tails
1 cup dry white wine or vermouth
1 bay leaf
4 black peppercorns
4 parsley stems
7 cups water

1. Heat the oil in a large soup pot over medium heat. Add the onion, leek, and fennel; sauté for 5 minutes, stirring occasionally.
2. Increase the heat to medium-high and add the garlic, fish parts, wine, bay leaf, peppercorns, parsley stems, and water, adding a bit more water if necessary to cover the bones.
3. Bring the stock to a gentle simmer and cook for 30 minutes, skimming any foam that rises to the top. Strain through a fine-mesh sieve and use within 3 days, or freeze for up to 3 months.

Dandelion Greens, Italian Sausage, and Fontina Cheese Pizza

Two 12-inch pizzas, 2 to 4 servings

Cultivated dandelion greens aren't just for salads. When they are sautéed in garlic-infused olive oil, their earthy, slightly bitter flavor shines, which counters the rich cow's milk cheese and Italian sausage in this unconventional pizza recipe. I use a locally made fontina cheese from Willamette Valley Cheese Company. Use whatever locally made cheese you like, but remember that one with a strong flavor will work best with the other assertive flavors in this recipe.

Baking pizza on preheated baking tiles or a pizza stone makes the crust perfectly crisp. They can be found at most kitchenware stores. If you don't have one, you can bake the pies on heavy baking sheets, but the crust will be paler and have less crunch.

FOR THE DOUGH:

¾ cup warm water
1 teaspoon honey
One .25-ounce packet yeast
1 tablespoon plus 1 teaspoon olive oil, divided
1 cup whole-wheat flour
1½ cups all-purpose flour
1 pinch salt

FOR THE TOPPING:

2 Italian sausages
1 bunch (6 to 8 ounces) dandelion greens
2 tablespoons olive oil, divided
1 tablespoon sliced garlic
Salt and freshly ground black pepper
2 tablespoons coarsely ground cornmeal, divided
6 ounces fontina or other strong-flavored cheese, cut into small cubes
Truffle oil, for garnish (optional)

1. Preheat the oven to 350°F. Place a baking stone on the center rack of oven. Combine the water, honey, and yeast in a large mixing bowl; allow it to sit for 3 minutes. Stir in 1 tablespoon of the oil, the flours, and the salt; knead until the dough is smooth and elastic, about 10 minutes by hand or 3 minutes with the dough hook of an electric mixer.

continued

2. Place the dough in a clean mixing bowl rubbed with the remaining oil, cover with plastic wrap, and allow it to rest in a warm place (about 72°F; near your oven is a good choice) until the dough has doubled in volume, about 1½ hours.
3. Meanwhile, prick the sausages a few times with a fork and place them in a small baking dish. Bake, turning once, until they are just cooked through, 20 to 25 minutes. Slice them ¼ inch thick.
4. Increase the oven temperature to 450°F. Wash the dandelion greens in a large bowl of cold water. Scoop the greens from the water, cut away the tough stems, and roughly chop the leaves into 1-inch pieces. Pat dry with paper towels.
5. Heat the oil in a large sauté pan over medium-high heat. Add the garlic and cook until it begins to brown. Remove the garlic with a fork and discard. Carefully add the dandelion greens to the hot garlic-infused oil and toss with tongs to wilt; cook for 30 seconds. Season with salt and pepper and set aside.
6. Cut the dough into 2 pieces. On a lightly floured surface, roll each piece into a 12-inch round. Sprinkle a baker's peel or inverted baking sheet with 1 tablespoon of the cornmeal and place one round of dough on top. Spread half the cheese over the dough, top with half the dandelion greens and half the sausage slices.
7. Use a decisive jerking motion to slide the pizza onto the baking stone in the oven. Bake until the crust is golden brown and the cheese is bubbly, about 10 minutes. Remove from oven with a pizza peel to a cutting board, drizzle with truffle oil, cut into wedges, and serve immediately. Repeat with second ball of dough.

Rice Vermicelli with Grilled Lemongrass Pork and Fresh Herbs

4 servings

This healthy Vietnamese-inspired noodle dish combines marinated grilled pork with cold rice noodles (called *bun* in Vietnamese) and mounds of crisp vegetables and herbs. It makes for a light but filling entrée—a great choice for dinner when the weather begins to get warm. Bun noodles are available at Asian markets and some grocery stores; they are often labeled "rice vermicelli."

FOR THE PORK SKEWERS:

1 pound pork loin
3 stalks lemongrass
1 bird chile*
1 garlic clove
3 tablespoons coconut milk
2 tablespoons fish sauce
2 tablespoons sweetened condensed milk
2 tablespoons sugar
1 teaspoon salt
1/4 teaspoon freshly ground black pepper
Bamboo skewers

FOR THE DIPPING SAUCE:

Juice of 1 lime
6 tablespoons fish sauce
3 tablespoons sugar
1 bird chile, chopped
2/3 cup water

FOR THE NOODLE BOWL:

1/2 head (about 3 cups) romaine lettuce, thinly shredded
1/2 small cucumber, halved lengthwise and thinly sliced
8 ounces rice vermicelli
1 cup bean sprouts
1 cup fresh mint leaves, stems removed
1 cup fresh cilantro leaves, stems removed
1/4 cup roasted peanuts, chopped
1 cup Pickled Daikon and Carrot Salad (see recipe, page 42)

1. Trim all the fat from the pork and freeze the pork for 30 minutes to make it easier to slice. Thinly slice it into 2- to 3-inch-long, ¼-inch-thick strips and put the strips in a large sealable plastic bag.
2. Cut the hard root end and dry grassy tips off of the lemongrass and discard. Peel the hard outer layers away and discard. Smack the stalk with the flat side of a knife and finely mince (you should have about ⅓ cup). Pound the lemongrass, bird chile, and garlic in a mortar and pestle until the mixture is a fairly uniform paste. (Alternatively, pulse the ingredients in a mini food processor.) Combine the paste with the coconut milk, fish sauce, condensed milk, sugar, salt, and pepper; add to the pork. Allow the meat to marinate refrigerated for at least 1 hour, but preferably overnight.
3. Preheat a grill over high heat. To make the dipping sauce, combine the lime juice, fish sauce, sugar, bird chile, and water in a bowl; stir to dissolve the sugar and set aside.
4. Bring a pot of water to a boil. Divide the lettuce, cucumber, and bean sprouts among 4 large bowls. Cook the vermicelli in the boiling water until just tender, about 3 minutes. Drain and rinse thoroughly with cold water until cool. Squeeze to remove excess liquid and place on top of the lettuce mixture.
5. Remove the pork from the marinade and thread it onto skewers without overcrowding. Grill the skewers until the pork is cooked through, about 3 minutes per side.
6. Place a few skewers on top of each bowl, top with the mint, cilantro, peanuts, and pickled daikon salad. Serve with individual bowls of dipping sauce.

* Use care when handling any chile pepper: use gloves and never touch your eyes or mouth while working with them. Bird chiles, also called Thai chiles, are small, 1- to 2-inch-long red and green peppers. The Lao women at my farmer's market sell the chiles in spring, summer, and fall in small bags of about fifty each. Fortunately, they keep well in the freezer, so you can pull out just a few when needed. You can also find them in Asian markets and some supermarkets. Red chili paste or chili flakes can be substituted if necessary.

Pickled Daikon and Carrot Salad

4½ cups

This recipe, inspired by the thin strands of pickled daikon and carrot frequently served in Vietnamese restaurants, is a great side dish for grilled meat or fish. Daikon is a member of the radish family, and looks something like a thick white carrot. It has a crisp, juicy flesh with less heat than smaller red radishes. Daikon does equally well raw in salads and cooked in stews and braises where their peppery bite mellows to a buttery earthiness.

I use a julienne peeler (see Resources) that looks like a little rake to create long, thin strands of daikon and carrot for this recipe. Use a mandoline or box grater if a julienne peeler is unavailable.

½ pound daikon, peeled
½ pound carrots, peeled
1⅔ cup water
1 cup white vinegar
1 teaspoon salt
¾ cup sugar
Juice of 1 lime

1. Cut the daikon and carrot into thin strands using a julienne peeler; place in a colander. Place a salad plate on top of the vegetables and allow them to drain for 30 minutes.
2. Bring the water, vinegar, salt, sugar, and lime juice to a simmer in a small saucepan. Stir to dissolve sugar.
3. Remove the plate from the vegetables; rinse them well with cold water and squeeze out excess moisture. Place the vegetables in a large bowl, toss with vinegar mixture and allow to marinate for 1 hour. Lift salad out of brine with a fork and serve. Leftover vegetables can be stored in a plastic container, covered in brine, for up to 2 weeks.

How to Choose: Daikon are at the juiciest and mellow best when the weather is cool—winter and early spring specifically. If possible, choose specimens that still have their peppery greens attached to guarantee freshness. Use the greens as you would other hearty braising greens. Pick daikon that have taut white skin with no sign of shriveling or softness. Peel and use within 4 days of purchase, before they begin to soften. Be sure to store unused portions in a sealed bag—their aroma can permeate your refrigerator quickly.

Lamb Stew with Baby Spring Vegetables (Navarin d'Agneau Printanier)

4 servings

Chef Pascal Sauton of Carafe makes this classic French preparation when the cute baby vegetables are just starting to come to the farmer's market in spring. He recommends using the smallest turnips available and baby carrots with a few inches of their tender stems still attached. Other young spring vegetables like fresh English peas, haricot verts (small green string beans), and patty pan squash can be used as well.

1½ pounds boneless lamb from the shoulder or leg
Salt and freshly ground black pepper
2 tablespoons olive oil, divided
1 cup finely chopped onions
4 garlic cloves, sliced
1½ cups dry white wine
4 tablespoons tomato paste
4 cups beef or lamb stock
6 parsley stems
3 thyme sprigs
1 bay leaf
16 pearl onions, unpeeled
1 tablespoon butter
1 tablespoon sugar
1 pound (about 10) small new potatoes, peeled and quartered
8 baby turnips, peeled and cut into bite-size pieces
8 baby carrots, peeled if necessary
3 tablespoons finely chopped parsley

1. Trim the lamb of any excess fat and cut the meat into 1-inch cubes; season with salt and pepper. Heat 1 tablespoon of the oil over medium-high heat in a Dutch oven or cast iron pot. Add a handful of meat and cook until it is well browned on two sides. Remove from the pan and set aside. Repeat with the remaining lamb and pour off fat.
2. Put the remaining oil into the pot, add the onions and garlic, and cook for 1 minute. Deglaze the pan with the wine, scraping the bottom of the pan to loosen any browned bits, and boil until the wine is almost evaporated, about 5 minutes.

continued

3. Stir in the tomato paste, lamb, and enough stock to nearly submerge the meat. Tie the parsley stems, thyme sprigs, and bay leaf together with kitchen twine and add to the pot. Reduce the heat, cover, and simmer gently until the lamb is very tender, 1½ hours. If the sauce is too thin, uncover the pot for the last half hour of cooking.
4. While the lamb cooks, prepare the pearl onions. Bring a medium saucepan of salted water to a boil. Add the onions and cook for 1 minute. Remove them with a slotted spoon, reserving the liquid, and then slide off their skins. Melt the butter in a small sauté pan over medium-high heat, add the onions and sugar, and cook until they begin to caramelize, about 5 minutes; set aside.
5. Add the potatoes to the boiling water and cook until they are almost tender, about 10 minutes. Remove them with a slotted spoon, reserving the liquid, and transfer them to the lamb mixture. Cook the turnips and then the carrots in the boiling water until they are almost tender, about 10 minutes each. Remove them in turn with a slotted spoon and transfer to the lamb mixture.
6. Divide the stew among 4 bowls and garnish with the pearl onions and parsley.

How to Choose: Potatoes are sometimes referred to as either waxy or floury. Waxy potatoes (Yukon golds, fingerlings, Yellow Finnish) have a lower starch and higher moisture content and have a waxy feel when they are sliced after boiling or steaming. They hold their shape when cooked in liquid, so they're ideal for stew or potato salad. Floury potatoes (russets, Idaho) have a higher starch content and a drier flesh that tends to melt when cooked in liquid, so they're best baked or fried.

Strawberry Shortcakes with Lemon Curd Cream

8 servings

Adapted from a recipe by Pastry Chef Melissa Lehmkuhl of ROUX in Portland, this recipe is not your average strawberry shortcake. Imagine airy orange-scented cakes, whipped cream enriched with homemade lemon curd, and the sweetness of fresh strawberries coaxed with honey, and you'll begin to understand the heights that shortcake can reach. The lemon curd recipe makes enough for the filling plus leftovers to spread on muffins or scones.

FOR THE SHORTCAKES:

- 1/2 cup sugar
- 3 cups all-purpose flour
- 1 tablespoon plus 1 teaspoon baking powder
- 3/4 teaspoon salt
- 1/4 cup (1/2 stick) cold unsalted butter, cut into 1/2-inch pieces
- 2 tablespoons shortening
- Zest of 1 orange
- 2 cups whipping cream

FOR THE LEMON CURD:

- 1 cup plus 1 tablespoon sugar, divided
- 6 egg yolks
- 1/2 cup fresh juice from 2 large lemons
- Zest of 2 lemons
- 1/2 cup (1 stick) cold unsalted butter, cut into 1/2-inch pieces
- 2 cups cold whipping cream

FOR ASSEMBLY:

- 2 pints strawberries, hulled and quartered
- 3 tablespoons local honey

1. To make the shortcakes, pulse the sugar, flour, baking powder, and salt in a food processor. Add the butter, shortening, and orange zest, and pulse until the fats are in pieces no larger than small peas. (Alternatively, whisk the dry ingredients and cut the fats and zest into the flour with a pastry blender or your fingers.) Pour mixture into a large mixing bowl. Gradually add the cream and stir with a rubber spatula until the dough starts to come together. (You may not need all the cream.)

▸ *continued*

2. Line a baking sheet with parchment and set aside. Place the dough on a lightly floured surface and gently knead for about 5 folds. Roll the dough into a round about 1 to 1½ inches thick. Using a floured 3-inch cutter or water glass, cut out 6 rounds. Gather the dough scraps together to form 2 more rounds. Transfer to the prepared baking sheet. Freeze the rounds until firm, about 1 hour. Meanwhile, preheat the oven to 400°F.
3. Bake the shortcakes for 15 minutes; reduce the temperature to 350°F and continue to bake until they are golden brown and set in the center, about 10 minutes. (The shortcakes can be made ahead and kept at room temperature in an airtight container for up to 2 days.)
4. To make the lemon curd, whisk 1 cup of the sugar, egg yolks, lemon juice, and lemon zest in a stainless steel bowl. Bring a saucepan of water to a bare simmer and set the bowl with the egg yolk mixture over the water, making sure the bottom of the bowl does not touch the water. Cook, stirring frequently, until the mixture has thickened to the consistency of mayonnaise, about 30 minutes.
5. Remove the bowl and gradually whisk in the butter. Strain the curd through a fine-mesh sieve and allow to cool at room temperature. When cooled, whip the cream with the remaining sugar until soft peaks form. Gently fold in ¼ cup of the lemon curd or more to taste, and whip again until medium peaks form.
6. To assemble, hull and slice the strawberries; toss with the honey in a small bowl. Split the shortcakes widthwise and arrange on serving plates. Spoon the strawberries generously over the bottoms, top with the lemon curd cream, replace the tops, and serve.

How to Choose: Though I buy organic whenever I can, some folks don't have the resources or access to buy organic produce every day. However, I strongly caution you to buy organic strawberries. Conventionally raised strawberries are one of the most heavily contaminated foods in the United States, according to a report from the nonprofit organization Environmental Working Group. Beyond the frightening amount of pesticides sprayed on the fruit, the best reason to buy local, organic strawberries is the taste. Since they're not grown to be shipped to far-off lands, local berries can ripen on the vine to become sweet and juicy, attributes that no crunchy, factory-farmed berry could ever deliver.

Lemongrass and Thai Basil Sorbet

1 quart

You'll find lemongrass nearly year-round at grocery stores and some farmer's markets, but its herbaceous, lemony flavor is most reminiscent of the fresh flavors of spring. In this refreshing sorbet recipe, sugar water, lemon juice, and basil are combined to make a pale pink icy treat that tastes like springtime in a bowl. Purple-stemmed Thai basil adds a slightly anise-like flavor. If you can't find it, try the recipe with fresh mint or lemon verbena leaves instead.

Those without ice cream makers can store the mixture in a plastic container, freeze it for 4 hours or until set, and then rake the sorbet with a fork to break it up, making something akin to an Italian granita.

⅓ cup minced fresh lemongrass (see instructions, page 40)
1 cup sugar
3 cups water
¼ cup juice from 1 large lemon
1 teaspoon finely chopped Thai basil leaves
1 egg white, whipped until frothy

1. Combine the lemongrass and sugar in a food processor and process until the mixture is a coarse paste, scraping down the sides of the work bowl once or twice. (Alternatively, pound the lemongrass in a mortar and pestle to a rough paste and combine with sugar in a large bowl.)
2. Add the water to the work bowl and process until the mixture is combined, about 15 seconds. Transfer to a medium saucepan and bring to a boil over high heat. Turn off the heat and remove the saucepan from the stove. Cover and allow the mixture to steep for 20 minutes.
3. Strain the mixture through a fine-mesh sieve and refrigerate it until it is cold, about 1 hour. Stir the lemon juice into the mixture and place it in an ice cream maker. Process according to manufacturer's instructions. When the sorbet is half frozen, add the basil and egg white. (The egg white keeps the sorbet soft and scoopable after storing. If you have any concerns about using raw egg, you can omit it.) Continue to process until the sorbet is frozen. Store the sorbet in the freezer in an airtight container for up to 3 months. Allow it to warm slightly at room temperature before serving.

How to Choose: Buy lemongrass stalks that have full bulbs at the base and fresh-looking green or yellow-green tips. Don't buy it if it has become brown or brittle; it should look plump and smell fragrant. Refrigerate lemongrass in a plastic bag for up to 2 weeks.

Rhubarb Streusel Tart with Brown Sugar–Sour Cream Ice Cream

One 9-inch tart or six 4¾-inch tartlets

There's a collective sigh of relief in early spring when crimson stalks of rhubarb arrive at the farmer's markets—the first harbinger of spring. This tart is adapted from a recipe courtesy of Vitaly Paley, chef-owner of Paley's Place in Portland.

FOR THE CRUST:

- 1½ cups all-purpose flour
- ¼ cup sugar
- ¼ teaspoon kosher salt
- ½ cup (1 stick) cold unsalted butter, cut into ½-inch pieces
- 2 egg yolks

FOR THE STREUSEL:

- 6 tablespoons cold unsalted butter, cut into ½-inch pieces
- 2½ tablespoons almond paste or marzipan
- ½ cup sugar
- ⅔ cup all-purpose flour
- 1 teaspoon ground cinnamon

FOR THE FILLING:

- 1½ pounds (about 6 cups) rhubarb, thinly sliced
- 1 cup brown sugar
- 1½ teaspoons ground cinnamon
- 1 quart Brown Sugar–Sour Cream Ice Cream (see recipe, page 51)

1. To make the crust, blend the flour, sugar, salt, and butter in a food processor or an electric mixer with the paddle attachment until the butter lumps are no larger than peas. Whisk the egg yolks in a small measuring cup and add enough water to make ¼ cup liquid; add to flour mixture. Mix until the dough just starts to come together. Gather the dough, shape into a disc, and wrap in plastic wrap. Chill for at least 1 hour or up to 3 days.
2. To make the streusel, combine the butter, almond paste, sugar, flour, and cinnamon in a food processor and process until the mixture is in fine crumbles. (Alternatively, blend with a pastry blender.) Refrigerate until needed.

continued

3. Allow the dough to stand at room temperature for 5 minutes. Roll on a lightly floured surface into a ⅛-inch-thick disc, frequently rotating the dough to prevent sticking. Transfer to a 9-inch tart pan with removable bottom or into 6 tartlet pans. Ease the dough into the pan, fitting it to the pan's contour with fingertips, leaving some dough hanging over the edges. Trim the pastry edges by rolling the pin over the rim and discard trimmings. Freeze the shell until firm, about 30 minutes.
4. Preheat the oven to 375°F.
5. Make the rhubarb filling by combining the rhubarb, brown sugar, and cinnamon in a large sauté pan. Cook over medium heat, stirring frequently, until the rhubarb is fall-apart tender, about 10 minutes.
6. Fill the tart shell with the rhubarb mixture to within ½ inch from the top of the crust. Sprinkle on the streusel and transfer to a baking sheet. Bake until the streusel is golden brown and the filling is bubbly, about 45 minutes for the tart, or 25 to 30 minutes for the tartlets. Transfer tart shell to a wire rack and cool completely. Using a small sharp knife, gently loosen the crust from sides of pan. Push up pan bottom to release tart. Serve warm with the ice cream.

Brown Sugar–Sour Cream Ice Cream

1 quart

2 cups half-and-half

1¼ cups brown sugar

8 egg yolks

2 cups sour cream

1. In a small saucepan, scald the half-and-half over medium-low heat until hot.
2. Whisk the brown sugar and egg yolks together in a medium bowl. Slowly whisk in the half-and-half.
3. Return the mixture to the saucepan and cook over medium-low heat, stirring constantly with a rubber spatula until the mixture thickens enough to coat it, about 5 minutes.
4. Strain the mixture through a fine-mesh sieve into a metal bowl. Refrigerate until cold, then whisk the sour cream into the half-and-half mixture and freeze in an ice cream maker according to manufacturer's instructions.

Arborio Rice Pudding with Oven-Dried Strawberry Preserves and Sugared Almonds

6 servings

Sophisticated and comforting at the same time, this rice pudding recipe contributed by Pastry Chef Michelle Vernier of Wildwood in Portland combines a classic dessert with the intense flavor of spring strawberries brought out by the simple oven-roasting method used. Make extra jam and freeze it for a midwinter brunch when you need a taste of berry goodness.

3 cups whole milk, divided
1 pinch salt
2 pinches ground cardamom
½ vanilla bean
⅔ cup Arborio rice
6 tablespoons sugar, divided
2 egg yolks
¼ cup mascarpone cheese
3 tablespoons heavy cream
1¼ cups Oven-Dried Strawberry Preserves (see recipe, opposite)
1 cup Sugared Almonds (see recipe, opposite)

1. Heat 2½ cups of the milk, salt, and cardamom in a saucepan over low heat. Scrape the vanilla bean with a small paring knife to remove the sticky black seeds, and add them and the pod to the saucepan. Continue to cook until the mixture is warm. Meanwhile, rinse the rice in a large bowl of cold water, swishing it to remove the excess starch; drain and repeat. Drain the rice again and add it to the milk mixture, bring to a gentle simmer over medium-low heat, and cook for 15 minutes, stirring frequently. Reduce the heat to low and continue to cook, stirring occasionally, until the rice is tender and has absorbed most of the liquid, about 30 minutes more.
2. In a medium mixing bowl, whisk together 5 tablespoons of the sugar, egg yolks, and remaining milk. Add 1 cup of the rice mixture and whisk to combine; pour into the saucepan with the rice and cook over medium-low heat, stirring constantly until slightly thickened, about 3 minutes.
3. Transfer rice mixture to a large bowl and allow to cool for 15 minutes at room temperature, stirring occasionally to prevent skin from forming on the surface. Press a piece of plastic wrap on top of the pudding and refrigerate until cold.
4. In a small bowl, beat the mascarpone, heavy cream, and the remaining sugar until soft peaks form. Fold the cheese mixture into the rice pudding with a rubber spatula and divide among 6 dessert cups. Top with the preserves and almonds, and serve.

Oven-Dried Strawberry Preserves

1¼ cups

1 pint (2½ cups) strawberries, cleaned, hulled, and thinly sliced

1 cup sugar

1 teaspoon lemon juice

1. Preheat the oven to 200°F. Combine the strawberries, sugar, and lemon juice in a small saucepan and allow to macerate for 10 minutes. Bring the mixture to a gentle simmer over medium-low heat, stirring frequently.
2. Transfer the mixture to a rimmed baking sheet and bake, stirring every 20 minutes until it is thick and jammy, about 2 hours. Preserves can be made ahead, stored in an airtight container, and refrigerated for up to 1 week, or frozen for several months.

Sugared Almonds

1 cup

½ egg white

1 cup sliced almonds

¼ cup sugar

Preheat the oven to 350°F. Spray a small baking sheet with nonstick cooking spray. In a small bowl, whisk the egg white with a fork until light and foamy. Add the almonds and sugar and toss to combine. Spread the almonds on a baking sheet and bake until golden brown and crispy, stirring occasionally, about 10 minutes.

SUMMER

MAYBE FEEDING FRENZY ISN'T THE RIGHT PHRASE, but the buzz coming from the busy farmers and eager shoppers is almost tangible. Every week brings new crops to be excited about; it starts with sweet black cherries for muffins, little tomatoes for roasting, and slender zucchini to stuff. As the days grow hotter, the tomatoes grow bigger, the tomatillos fatter, and the eggplant plumper. The dining room is abandoned for the outdoor patio and cooking becomes more laissez faire. The flavors are so vivid that we hardly need to do anything to make great food. The grill gets a workout with a constant rotation of juicy flank steaks for fajitas, gingery grilled chicken skewers, and platters of glowing ripe vegetables. Life is easy, but it's time to think ahead to leaner times and start "putting by" peach and fig jams, roasted peppers, basil pesto, and oven-dried tomatoes so we can have a taste of summer when the winter winds begin to blow.

meet the producer

It's June 12 and Michael Paine, owner of Gaining Ground Farm, is getting ready for his first CSA drop of the season. Paine, a thirty-something with a full reddish beard and piercing blue eyes, looks more leprechaun than farmer as he dashes among the tables of produce he's set up in the driveway of a home in Portland's Sullivan's Gulch neighborhood. As his CSA farm share members arrive, there's a slight first-day-of-school feeling hanging in the air. They're excited but slightly coy since they haven't seen their farmer since the previous October. Michael's young interns, Emily, Christine, and Matt, break the ice by serving crackers and fresh goat cheese made by a neighboring farmer. They shake hands with every adult, kid, and dog, checking names on a clipboard as they meet.

A small dry-erase board leaned against one table lists the week's share for each family: one bunch of radishes, a half pound of fluffy baby lettuce leaves, two heads of bok choy, two pints of strawberries, one small bunch of lavender, and one pound of snap peas so sweet even the children are gobbling them up by the fistful. All the produce is artfully arranged—vegetables are cascading out of baskets—making this event seem like a micro–farmer's market.

As more CSA members arrive, the vibe changes to that of a block party as they greet Michael with bear hugs. He chats at length with each young family, answering inquiries about the farm, the produce, and the whereabouts of his pregnant wife, Jill, who is on her way from her day job. He's beaming as if there's no place he'd rather be. As he explains it, this is what being a farmer is about. "Every day is a long day, but there's real joy seeing the family who's going to eat your lettuce that day, or the kid that's stoked to grab his family's share and ask me if I'll bring extra kale for him next week. This is the best part of farming, right here in this driveway."

A day later, sitting at a large farmhouse table in the Paines' kitchen, we discuss what made Michael want to be a farmer at a time when small farms are disappearing. It began during a stint as a Peace Corps volunteer in Lesotho, the land-locked country surrounded by South Africa.

"Being in that agrarian landscape working with subsistence farmers was so new and amazing to me," he explains.

It was also a reality check. An antiapartheid stronghold, aid money poured into Lesotho in the late 1980s, but Paine was shocked at the ineffectiveness of most agricultural projects run by aid organizations. "The landscape was riddled with these broken-down visions of how to help people that weren't helpful. Clearly, big decisions were being made by people who didn't know anything at all about farming, and those decisions had a huge impact on those that survived by farming."

That experience, along with a farming stint in Costa Rica, led Paine to UC Davis for a master's program in international agricultural development so he could begin a career in informed policy-making. But the fields continued to call.

After school, Michael and Jill came to Oregon hoping to buy land to start their own small farm. In spite of finding the perfect plot of land about an hour west of Portland in the fertile Willamette Valley, the Paines were met with heartbreaking difficulty as they tried to get a loan. Banks in the area are extremely reluctant to lend to anyone interested in farming.

"If you have good credit and a good business plan, and you're going to produce food for the community, people should be bending over backwards to give you a loan at a good interest rate. We need more farmers, not hurdles for them to jump over, but that just wasn't the case," Jill points out.

After several weeks of touch-and-go maneuvering, a loan came through and Gaining Ground Farm was born. Four years later and the Paines are indeed gaining ground, serving forty-plus families in their farm share program and maintaining a successful booth at the Saturday farmer's market in Portland. As for policy-making, Michael may not be a big player in international agricultural policy, but he's effecting change in his own community by being a member of Portland's Food Policy Committee—an advisory committee that advocates for land use, education, and infrastructure changes to secure affordable, local, and sustainably grown food in the Portland area.

As I listened to the Paine's story over a few pale ales and a delicious pie Jill whipped up with strawberries from the farm, it became very clear that farmers like Michael and Jill can prove the skeptical loan officers of the world wrong: it is possible to start up a small farm and thrive. All you need is passion, vision, and a strong back.

Prosciutto-Wrapped Figs

6 servings

I had grilled figs for the first time at a potluck barbecue some years ago. Though some of us spent hours making complex salads and marinating meats, a butcher friend of ours showed up late, wrapped some figs in prosciutto, and tossed them on the grill, a beer in hand the whole time. We were all blown away!

12 ripe Mission figs
12 thin slices prosciutto, halved lengthwise
Toothpicks for securing (optional)
1 tablespoon good-quality balsamic vinegar
Freshly ground black pepper

1. Preheat the grill; set to high if using a gas grill. Halve figs lengthwise and wrap each half with 1 piece of prosciutto. The moisture from the prosciutto should make it adhere to itself and the fig; use the toothpicks if necessary.
2. When the grill is very hot, put the figs on the grill. Cook until the prosciutto is singed slightly, about 2 minutes; carefully turn over and grill for 2 more minutes.
3. Transfer the figs to a serving platter, drizzle sparingly with the vinegar, sprinkle with pepper, and serve.

Sicilian Eggplant Spread with Crostini

6 servings

I know many people do not care for eggplant, and it's no wonder—they've been subjected to bitter, mass-produced specimens that have none of the creamy goodness of a well-grown eggplant. The complex flavor and nearly melted texture of eggplant in this recipe has made more than one eggplant-hater change their tune.

½ cup plus 1 tablespoon olive oil, divided
1 cup chopped onion
3 tablespoons pine nuts
3 tablespoons dried currants or raisins
½ teaspoon dried oregano
3 large garlic cloves, sliced
1 pound (4½ cups) eggplant, cut into ½-inch cubes
1 teaspoon sugar
½ teaspoon ground cinnamon
1 teaspoon unsweetened cocoa powder
1 cup tomato sauce
3 tablespoons balsamic vinegar
Salt and freshly ground black pepper
1 loaf of rustic French bread, sliced ¼ inch thick

1. Preheat the oven to 350°F. Heat ½ cup of the oil in a large sauté pan over medium-high heat; add the onion, pine nuts, currants, and oregano. Cook until the onion is soft and translucent, about 8 minutes.
2. Reduce the heat to medium; add the garlic, eggplant, sugar, cinnamon, and cocoa. Cook, stirring frequently, until the eggplant begins to brown and becomes soft around the edges, about 15 minutes.
3. Add the tomato sauce and vinegar, cover, and simmer until the eggplant is very tender, about 30 minutes. Season with salt and pepper and set aside for at least 1 hour to meld flavors.
4. Meanwhile, place the bread slices in a single layer on 2 baking sheets. Lightly brush them with the remaining oil and sprinkle lightly with salt and pepper. Bake just until the bread is crisp and golden brown around the edges, about 15 minutes. Serve warm with eggplant mixture.

Heirloom Tomato Panzanella

6 servings

Panzanella is a thrifty Italian dish that uses day-old bread and plentiful late-summer tomatoes to make a filling salad. Several colors of heirloom tomatoes at the base of the salad add to the visual appeal. If you're preparing this ahead, don't mix the bread with the tomatoes and vinaigrette until just before serving or the bread will become mushy.

1 small loaf (10 ounces) rustic bread
1 garlic clove, peeled
½ cup kalamata olives
¼ cup plus 2 tablespoons extra virgin olive oil, divided
Salt and freshly ground black pepper
2½ pounds heirloom tomatoes
2 cups baby arugula
1 tablespoon minced shallots
2 tablespoons balsamic vinegar
½ teaspoon Dijon mustard

1. Preheat the oven to 375°F. Slice the tough bottom crust off the bread and discard. Rub the loaf with the garlic to subtly flavor it. Cut the bread into 2-inch pieces (you should have about 6 cups) and place on a rimmed baking sheet with the olives. Toss with 2 tablespoons of the oil, salt, and pepper. Bake until the cubes are crisp, about 15 to 20 minutes, stirring once.
2. Cut the core from each tomato with a paring knife and discard. With a sharp serrated knife, slice the tomatoes ½ inch thick. Place 4 or 5 slices in a concentric circle on 4 salad plates. Sprinkle with salt and pepper.
3. Chop enough of the remaining tomato slices to measure 1 cup and put in a large bowl with the bread cubes, olives, and arugula. Divide any remaining tomato slices among the plates.
4. Combine the shallots, vinegar, and mustard in a small bowl. Slowly whisk in the remaining oil.
5. Toss the bread cube mixture with enough shallot dressing to coat the arugula; season with salt and pepper to taste. Pile on top of the sliced tomatoes and serve.

Spicy Shrimp and Cucumber Salad

4 servings

This Thai-inspired salad is light, yet substantial enough to serve as a main course on balmy nights when a meal on the patio or a picnic is in order. The vibrant lime juice dressing has the classic Thai balance of chile pepper heat, salty fish sauce, sour lime, and sugar, a combination that dances on the tongue. The salad itself is very adaptable; you can substitute chopped rotisserie chicken for the shrimp, or add whatever produce looks good at the market—tomatoes, green beans, or diced mango all work well.

FOR THE DRESSING:

1 large garlic clove, peeled
1 to 2 small red bird chiles (see *, page 40)
4 tablespoons lime juice
3 tablespoons fish sauce
2 teaspoons sugar

FOR THE SALAD:

8 cups water
1 pound shrimp, peeled, deveined, tail left intact
Ice water
1 cucumber, halved and thinly sliced
1 medium shallot, thinly sliced
½ cup fresh mint leaves
½ cup cilantro leaves
½ cup fried shallots, sliced* (optional)

1. Grind the garlic and bird chiles in a mortar and pestle or finely chop into a paste; put in a small mixing bowl. Add the lime juice, fish sauce, and sugar; whisk to dissolve the sugar.
2. Bring the water to a boil in a medium saucepan. Add the shrimp and cook until they curl and turn pink, about 1 minute. Remove with a slotted spoon and plunge into the ice water to stop them from overcooking. Drain.
3. Combine the shrimp, cucumber, shallot, mint, and cilantro with the dressing. Sprinkle with the fried shallots and serve.

* Sliced fried shallots are sold in plastic jars at most Asian markets. To make them yourself, heat 2 cups of vegetable oil in a small saucepan over high heat until hot. Thinly slice 3 to 4 shallots, toss them in a few tablespoons of cornstarch, shake off the excess, and fry in the oil until crisp and golden brown. Remove and drain on paper towels. Use immediately.

French Sorrel and Mission Fig Salad with Crème Fraîche Vinaigrette

4 servings

Maria Hines, chef-owner of Tilth in Seattle, used her homegrown French sorrel when she first served this salad at her restaurant. Thanks to her close connection to the farmers she buys from, Full Circle Farm is now growing French sorrel for Chef Hines. The bite-size, shield-shaped leaves have a tart, lemony flavor that is tempered here with creamy vinaigrette, figs, and melon. French sorrel is becoming more common at farmer's markets; you can use garden sorrel or spinach as a substitute (add a tablespoon of lemon juice to the vinaigrette if using spinach).

½ cup crème fraîche or sour cream
2½ tablespoons red wine vinegar
2 tablespoons minced chives
Salt and freshly ground black pepper
1 cup (4 ounces) diced heirloom melon such as Charentais
3½ cups (6 ounces) French sorrel, tough stems removed
½ cup hazelnuts, toasted, skinned, and chopped (see instructions, page 146)
4 Mission figs, quartered lengthwise

1. Whisk the crème fraîche, vinegar, and chives in a small bowl. Season with salt and pepper.
2. Divide the melon among 4 chilled salad plates. Toss the sorrel and hazelnuts in a large bowl with enough crème fraîche mixture to lightly coat the leaves.
3. Pile the salad on top of the melon; decorate the plates with the figs and serve.

How to Choose: French sorrel is best when the leaves are young and succulent. Choose bunches with bright, crisp leaves; avoid those with woody stems or wilted, yellowing leaves. Wash in a sink full of cool water and spin or pat dry. Loosely wrap the leaves in paper towels and store in a plastic bag in the vegetable keeper for up to 3 days.

Garden sorrel has long, spear-shaped leaves tinged with red when very young. Though garden sorrel does not have the crisp, lemon flavor of French sorrel, the two are generally interchangeable. Sorrel is commonly cooked with cream for a tart sauce that pairs nicely with wild salmon; it's also good pureed with chicken stock, potatoes, and cream for soup.

Melon Salad with Ricotta Salata and Lemon Salt

4 servings

Chef Ande Janousek of Carmelita in Seattle writes her menus based on what organic farmers and foragers bring to her. "I don't write my menu until I've talked to my growers to see what's coming from their farms," she says. Her model is ideal for you, too: go to the market and *then* decide what you're going to cook.

For this salad recipe, Chef Janousek shaves several kinds of melons when they are at their peak with a vegetable peeler into colorful noodle-like lengths and decorates the plate with zig zags of sweet balsamic reduction for a dazzling presentation. The recipe makes enough lemon salt and balsamic reduction to use in other dishes. Store the salt in an airtight container and sprinkle it on fish, chicken, and salads. The balsamic reduction will keep for a few months when stored in a small squeeze bottle or airtight container in the refrigerator; bring to room temperature before using.

2 lemons
1 tablespoon kosher salt
½ cup balsamic vinegar
1 teaspoon lemon juice
1 tablespoon extra virgin olive oil
1 pound melon (a variety is best)
5 large basil leaves, torn
2 cups mâche (also called lamb's lettuce) or mesclun greens
2 ounces ricotta salata*, crumbled

1. One day before you plan to serve the salad, zest the lemons over a dinner plate. Allow the zest to dehydrate overnight. Finely grind the zest and salt in a mortar and pestle or clean spice grinder until finely ground; set aside.
2. To make the balsamic reduction, simmer the vinegar in a small saucepan over medium-low heat until it is syrupy and coats a spoon. Cool to room temperature.
3. Whisk the lemon juice with the oil in a small bowl.
4. With a sharp vegetable peeler, peel thick slices of melon and shave them into long, thin strips. Arrange the strips in rumpled mounds on 4 salad plates.

▸ *continued*

5. Put the basil, mâche, ricotta salata, oil mixture, and a pinch of the lemon salt in a large bowl; toss gently to combine. Center one quarter of the mixture on top of each melon arrangement. Dip a fork into the balsamic reduction, flick quickly over each salad to make attractive Pollock-esque zigzags, and serve.

* Ricotta salata is an Italian sheep's milk cheese with a salty bite and semifirm texture. Feta or other sheep's milk cheese can be substituted.

How to Choose: Melons will soften after being plucked from the vine, but will never get any sweeter, so choose the ripest melon you can find. Leave the thumping of melons to the professionals; it takes a trained ear to "hear" ripeness. Instead, smell the blossom end opposite the "belly button" of the melon; it should smell sweet and melony. Gently press the melon; it should have a slight give. When choosing a watermelon, look for a ground spot—where the melon rested on the ground. A yellowish hue indicates ripeness; a greenish or white spot indicates that the melon was picked too young.

Chilled Cucumber Soup with Salad Burnet

4 to 6 servings

This chilled soup recipe, contributed by Chef Scott Dolich of Park Kitchen in Portland, is a delicious, light start to a special midsummer meal. Chef Dolich strives to use ingredients that travel as few miles as possible, as with the salad burnet in this recipe—it's picked daily from Chef de Cuisine David Padberg's home garden. Its small scallop-edged leaves have a cucumber-like flavor that adds a cooling freshness to soups, salads, and dips. Occasionally, in warmer months I find it in bunches at farmer's markets, though I usually see it sold as a garden start. It is easy to grow in containers or your herb garden.

FOR THE CUCUMBER SOUP:

8 cups roughly diced burpless cucumber
1 cup sweet onion such as Walla Walla, chopped
1 medium garlic clove, center green sprout removed, or 4 garlic spears, chopped
½ cup sesame seeds, toasted
½ cup Italian parsley leaves
Zest and juice of 3 limes
3 ounces firm tofu, diced
1 cup olive oil
Salt and freshly ground black pepper

FOR THE SALAD BURNET GARNISH:

1 ounce firm tofu
2½ tablespoons soymilk
Zest of 1 lime
¼ cup salad burnet leaves

1. Combine the cucumber, onion, garlic, sesame seeds, parsley, lime zest, and lime juice in a large mixing bowl. Allow the mixture to stand for 1 hour to meld flavors.
2. In a blender, blend the cucumber mixture and tofu in batches, slowly adding the oil in a slow, steady stream to create an emulsified mixture (it will look creamy). Strain through a fine-mesh sieve into a large serving bowl; chill for 1 hour.

▸ *continued*

3. To make the salad burnet garnish, put the tofu, soymilk, and lime zest in a blender; process for a smooth, yogurt-like consistency. Fold in the salad burnet.
4. Season the soup with salt and pepper and serve, passing the salad burnet cream separately as a garnish.

How to Choose: Burpless cucumbers are Asian hybrids with less bitterness than conventional cucumbers. Popular varieties include Sweet Slice, Tasty Green, and Garden Sweet. They're long and slender, with prickly bumps and dark green skins that do not need to be peeled. Choose heavy, slender cucumbers that are not waxed or oiled. They should have no soft spots and the ends should not be shriveled. Professor Todd C. Wehner at North Carolina State University determined that burpless cucumbers do indeed cause less "burpiness" than their conventional counterparts, but if you're unable to find them, seek out English or hothouse varieties, or halve everyday cucumbers lengthwise and scoop out the seeds before chopping.

Sweet Corn Chowder with Tomato and Basil

4 servings

This soup really shows off the rich flavor of corn at its peak. The chowder is creamy while managing to be relatively low in fat; the richness comes from the starchy corncob stock and potatoes. The tomato-basil garnish is a tasty but optional addition.

4 ears fresh yellow corn
4 cups chicken or vegetable stock
2 cups water
1 bay leaf
2 tablespoons butter
1 cup finely chopped onion
1 red or orange pepper, finely chopped
2 tablespoons all-purpose flour
1 pound Russet potatoes, peeled and cut into 2-inch chunks
1 teaspoon salt
1 pinch cayenne pepper
Salt and freshly ground black pepper
1 cup grated cheddar cheese
1 medium (1/2 cup) tomato, seeded and chopped
2 tablespoons freshly chopped basil
2 green onions, chopped

1. Shuck the corn. To shave the kernels from the cob, hold a cob upright at a slight angle on a cutting board and cut off the kernels with a sharp chef's knife, being careful not to cut the cob. Repeat with the remaining ears. Set the kernels aside.
2. Put the cobs, stock, water, and bay leaf in a large soup pot and bring to a boil over high heat. Cover, reduce the heat, and simmer for 30 minutes. Strain the broth into a large bowl and set aside; discard the corn cobs and bay leaf.
3. Put the pot over medium-high heat. Add the butter, onion, and pepper and then cook, stirring occasionally, until the onion is translucent, about 8 minutes.
4. Add the flour and cook for 1 minute, stirring constantly. Slowly stir in the warm broth and bring to a boil. Add half the corn kernels, potatoes, and salt; reduce the heat to medium-low. Cover and simmer until the potatoes are tender, about 20 minutes.

continued

5. Stir in the remaining corn kernels and cayenne pepper; cook 5 minutes. (If you prefer thicker chowder, smash some of the potatoes against the side of the pot to thicken.) Season with salt and pepper to taste. Remove from the stove and gradually whisk in the cheese until it melts completely.
6. In a small bowl combine the tomato, basil, and green onions. Ladle the soup into 4 bowls and gently spoon the tomato-basil garnish on top.

How to Choose: Look for corn that has bright green, fresh-looking husks and plump rows of kernels when you gently press through the husk. The silk should be bright and dry; the stalk end should be moist, not dry and chalky. Please don't peel back the husks to examine the corn: it dries out the kernels and renders the ear unsellable. Corn kernels convert their sugars to starches the moment they are picked, thus the midwestern rule: don't pick the corn until the cooking water is boiling. That's not possible for those of us without kitchen gardens, but it is good to keep in mind that the corn you buy should be eaten the day you buy it. If you can't, store it unshucked to help keep it fresh. Some purists store corn in the refrigerator in a bag set over a bowl of ice to keep it as fresh as possible.

Roasted Tomato Soup with Basil

4 servings

Take advantage of late-summer tomatoes by slow roasting and freezing them, and then digging them out in the late fall, long after tomatoes are done for the year. They are great stuffed with marinated feta as a cocktail nibble, as a pizza topping, or blended into a pasta sauce or soup, as in this recipe. I use inexpensive plum tomatoes; heirloom tomatoes can be used as well.

4 pounds ripe plum (Roma) tomatoes, halved
6 sprigs fresh herbs (a combination of thyme, oregano, and summer savory)
3 tablespoons olive oil
Salt and freshly ground black pepper
2 tablespoons butter
1 cup finely chopped onion
2 teaspoons minced garlic
3 cups chicken stock, mild vegetable stock, or water
1 bay leaf
½ cup heavy cream
1 cup fresh basil leaves

1. Preheat the oven to 200°F. Line a baking sheet with parchment paper.
2. Place the tomatoes cut side up on the prepared baking sheet. Distribute the herbs evenly over the tomatoes, drizzle with the oil, and sprinkle with salt and pepper. Bake until the tomatoes are shriveled but still plump, about 8 hours. The tomatoes can be frozen at this point: place them on baking sheets lined with parchment paper and freeze for 2 hours. When frozen, carefully transfer them to sealable plastic freezer bags and store in the freezer for up to 4 months.
3. Melt the butter in a large soup pot over medium heat. Add the onion and cook, stirring occasionally, until it is softened and beginning to brown, about 10 minutes. Add the garlic and cook for 1 minute.
4. Stir in the tomatoes, stock, and bay leaf. Increase the heat to medium-high and bring to a boil. Reduce the heat, cover, and simmer gently for 30 minutes, occasionally mashing the tomatoes with a wooden spoon.
5. Remove the bay leaf. Using a food mill or blender, puree the soup until smooth. (If you prefer a very silky texture, strain the pureed soup through a fine-mesh sieve.) Return the soup to the pot; add the cream and season with salt and pepper. Keep warm over low heat.
6. Stack the basil leaves stem-end toward you and roll cigar-style. Finely slice the leaves to create attractive ribbons. Ladle soup into 4 bowls, sprinkle basil over the top, and serve.

Heirloom Tomato Primer

An heirloom is any object with quality and value that is handed down from one generation to the next. It may come in and go out of favor; it may be forgotten or cast aside for more modern, flashy items; but an heirloom has a certain time-tested quality, a realness and connection to the past. Though there are multitudes of heirloom plants that have recently taken the gardening world by storm, the most popular is undoubtedly the heirloom tomato, and for good reason.

Americans lost real tomatoes for decades, casting aside the odd-shaped vine-ripened varieties for the uniformity of mealy orbs that could be shipped long distances and offered year-round.

These imposters are not picked when ripe (they pack and travel better when they're rock hard) and are tricked into turning red by a dose of ethylene gas.

Thankfully, those who could still remember the deliciousness of a Cherokee purple or the delicacy of a Green Zebra kept the tomato dream alive, and now we can grow our own real tomatoes or buy them in season at farmer's markets. Judging by the demand and the price they fetch, heirloom tomatoes will endure.

Choose tomatoes that have a good heft (they are juicier). Never refrigerate them or they will turn mealy and sad. Display them in your best wooden bowl as a centerpiece of old garden knowledge rediscovered.

1. **AMANA ORANGE:** These large golden-yellow to orange tomatoes have a rich, fruity flesh and minimal acidity. Their vibrant color makes them a showstopper sliced in salads or diced in gazpacho.

2. **BLACK KRIM:** Also called Black Crimson, these slightly flattened gems have a mahogany flesh with green shoulders. The firm fruit has a slightly salty finish, making it a nice garnish for burgers or grilled cheese sandwiches.

3. **MARVEL STRIPE:** These pretty, plump, yellow-orange tomatoes have showy crimson streaks, making them a good slicing tomato for salads. They have a thin skin and a juicy, sweet flavor that pairs nicely with feta cheese in Greek dishes.

4. **CHEROKEE PURPLE:** A stunning heirloom with deep burgundy flesh and forest green stripes on its shoulders. Their earthy flavor and tender texture shine when they are combined with a peppery olive oil and basil as a bruschetta topping.

5. **BRANDYWINE:** Cultivated from an Amish heirloom seed, the Brandywine's deep wine–colored skin reveals a big, beefy tomato that is perfectly suited for BLTs and tomato salads.

6. **GREEN ZEBRA:** The supermodel of heirloom tomatoes, the flashy yellow-and-green-striped flesh of this smallish tomato has a nice tang that lends itself to salsas and salads.

7. **MORTGAGE LIFTER:** A disease-tolerant deep red tomato, its sweet flavor and small number of seeds make it the perfect choice for layering with fresh mozzarella and basil in caprese salad.

8. **SUNGOLD:** A bit larger than cherry tomatoes, these are almost like candy in their sweetness, combined with a cheese-like richness. This is the tomato for those who think they don't like tomatoes.

9. **RED PEAR:** A small teardrop-shaped tomato with sweet fruit that is best quickly sautéed or eaten raw dipped in ranch dressing.

10. **PURPLE CHERRY:** These are sweet, with an almost crisp skin, tangy seeds, and a sharp finish.

11. **GARDEN PEACH:** These golden orbs have the color and soft fuzz of a peach. They are sweet with a pleasant, rich aftertaste. Try eating one out of your hand as you would an apple, or stuffing them with crab salad or flavored couscous.

End of Summer Quiche

4 to 6 servings

Sweet corn, smoky roasted red peppers, and tangy local goat cheese come together in this recipe with farm-fresh eggs to make an easy weeknight supper. You can make the basic recipe with many late-summer vegetables, from leftover grilled eggplant to quickly sautéed zucchini. Serve with a green salad or sliced melon.

2 tablespoons olive oil
1 small onion, sliced 1/2 inch thick
2 ears corn, shucked
One 9-inch baked pie crust
1 red bell pepper, roasted and chopped (see recipe, opposite)
2 ounces goat cheese, crumbled
2 large egg yolks, preferably free range
2 large eggs, preferably free range
1 cup half-and-half
1/2 teaspoon salt
1 pinch ground nutmeg
Freshly ground black pepper

1. Position the oven rack in the middle and preheat the oven to 350°F. Heat the oil in a medium sauté pan over medium-high heat, add the onion, and sauté, stirring occasionally, until the onion begins to caramelize, about 8 minutes.
2. To shave the kernels from the corn, hold a cob upright at a slight angle on a cutting board and cut off the kernels with a sharp chef's knife, being careful not to cut the cob. Add the kernels to the sauté pan and cook for 1 minute. Place the pie shell on a baking sheet; add the corn mixture, bell pepper, and goat cheese.
3. Whisk the egg yolks, eggs, half-and-half, salt, nutmeg, and a few grinds of pepper in a medium bowl. Pour mixture into the pie shell and bake for 25 to 30 minutes, until the edges are set and a knife inserted 1 inch from the edge comes out clean (the filling will continue to set after the quiche is removed from the oven). Allow the quiche to cool for 10 minutes before serving.

The Indispensable Jar of Roasted Red Bell Peppers

2 pints

No matter how many of these silky, smoky roasted peppers I have it never seems to be enough. Use them in quick kitchen-cupboard pasta salads, sandwiches, pasta sauces, and as a simple side to grilled steak. I stockpile red bell peppers when they are at their peak in late summer, roast them on the grill or gas stove, and store them submerged in olive oil in the refrigerator (or freeze a few bags for later). When the peppers are gone, I use the oil in salad dressings and sautés.

4 large red bell peppers with flat, uniform sides
Olive oil

1. Lay the peppers directly on gas burners over medium-high heat, grill over hot coals, or broil on a baking sheet 2 inches from the broiler element.
2. Roast the peppers, turning occasionally with tongs, until all the skins are blistered and charred, about 10 minutes (15 minutes if broiling).
3. Put the peppers in a large bowl, cover with plastic wrap, and allow them to steam for 20 minutes. Rub off the skins with your fingers. Carefully open them and pull out the seeds and pale ribs; remove the stems. Quickly rinse the peppers to remove any remaining seeds and blackened skin. Discard the skins, seeds, ribs, and stems.
4. Slice the peppers into quarters and pack them into a clean jar or plastic container; they should fit snugly. Pour in oil to cover the peppers completely. Be sure no parts of the peppers are peeking out of the oil or they will spoil more quickly. Refrigerate and keep for 2 to 3 weeks. They can also be roasted as described, packed without oil into freezer bags, and kept frozen for up to 3 months.

Grilled Vegetable Galette

4 main course servings

I suffer from grill guilt. I love the flavor that mesquite charcoal infuses into food, but it seems such a shame to burn all that charcoal for just a few steaks or chicken skewers. To use every moment of the glowing embers, I throw on spare vegetables after I'm done grilling. This rustic, open-faced tart came together from just such an impulse.

FOR THE CRUST:

1 cup all-purpose flour
¼ cup fine cornmeal
1 teaspoon sugar
½ teaspoon salt
7 tablespoons cold unsalted butter, cut into small pieces
3 tablespoons plain full-fat yogurt
¼ cup cold water

FOR THE FILLING:

1 medium (about 1 pound) eggplant, sliced into ½-inch-thick rounds
1 cup olive oil, divided
Salt and freshly ground black pepper
6 ounces zucchini, sliced at an angle ½ inch thick
1 medium portobello mushroom
4 ounces soft cow's milk cheese such as Havarti, fontina, or Fontal
1 cup roasted red bell peppers (see recipe, page 75)
1 egg yolk
1 teaspoon water

1. Put the flour, cornmeal, sugar, salt, and butter in a food processor or large mixing bowl. Pulse or work in the butter with a pastry blender until the butter is no larger than small peas. In a small bowl, stir the yogurt and cold water with a fork and then add to the flour mixture. Fold in with a rubber spatula until the dough just comes together. Squeeze it together with your hands and transfer to plastic wrap. Form the dough into a disc, wrap tightly, and refrigerate for at least 2 hours.

2. Preheat the grill. (Alternatively, roast the vegetables in a single layer on parchment-lined baking sheets at 400°F or cook on the stove in a grill pan over high heat.) Brush the eggplant liberally on both sides with a little less than ½ cup of the oil. Sprinkle with salt and pepper, and grill until eggplant is tender when pierced with a fork and edges are translucent, about 4 minutes per side, spreading out coals to reduce heat if the slices begin to burn. Repeat with the zucchini, brushing with oil, seasoning with salt and pepper, and grilling slices until they are still crisp-tender, about 1 minute per side. Set the vegetables aside.
3. Remove the stem from the mushroom and scrape off the black quills on the underside of the cap. Brush with the remaining oil, season with salt and pepper, and grill until tender, about 4 minutes per side. Slice into strips.
4. Preheat the oven to 375°F and line a baking sheet with parchment paper. Remove dough from refrigerator and let rest for 5 minutes at room temperature. On a lightly floured surface, roll the dough into a 12-inch round; carefully transfer it to the prepared baking sheet.
5. Cut the cheese into thin slices and place in the center of the dough; top with the grilled vegetables and bell peppers, leaving a 2-inch border around the edges. Bring the edges of the dough up and over the outer edge of the vegetables; lightly press the dough together where the edges meet. The galette is meant to look rustic; just let the edges overlap each other and try not to fuss with it too much or the dough will toughen.
6. Whisk the egg yolk, water, and a pinch of salt; brush evenly over the dough. Bake until golden brown, about 45 minutes. Serve hot or at room temperature.

How to Choose: Several zucchini varieties beyond the common deep green type abound. Sunny yellow zucchini have loads of flavor, orb-shaped globe zucchini have a rich custardy flesh, and the light green–and-white-striped Middle Eastern variety have a firm flesh that fries well. Whichever zucchini you choose, look for relatively small specimens with shiny skin and no shriveled or browning areas. Any nicks in zucchini skin will cause spoilage more quickly.

Pesto Pasta Genovese

4 main course servings, 6 side dish servings

Pesto originates in Liguria, in the northwest of Italy, where it is taken very seriously. Though there are endless ingredient variations (pine nuts, walnuts, oregano, no cheese), most Ligurians will agree that the slow bruising and smashing of ingredients in a heavy mortar and pestle yields a better pesto than pureeing the basil in a food processor or blender with a steel blade. I encourage you to pound pesto by hand at least once so you can taste the difference. Freeze pesto flat in an airtight sealable freezer bag for up to 3 months. Just break off a piece while it's still frozen whenever you need a little pesto fix.

Traditionally, this dish is made with *trofie*, 2-inch-long pasta twists. Here it's corkscrew-shape pasta; it's easier to find, catches the sauce well, and looks lovely heaped into a bowl for a picnic or barbecue.

2 cups (about 1 ounce) fresh basil leaves
1 pinch sea salt
½ teaspoon fresh lemon juice
1 large garlic clove, peeled
¾ cup extra virgin olive oil
½ cup grated Parmesan cheese
¼ cup grated Pecorino Romano cheese
Salt and freshly ground black pepper
1 pound Yukon gold potatoes, peeled and cut into 1-inch chunks
8 ounces dried fusilli or trofie pasta
½ pound thin green beans, stem ends snapped off

1. If necessary, wipe the basil with a moistened paper towel to remove any dirt. (Rinsing the leaves can wash away some of their aromatic oils.) Remove the leaves from their stems and tear the leaves into small pieces.
2. Place a handful of leaves in a large stone or wood mortar with the salt and lemon juice. Smash and grind the leaves against the bottom of the mortar, gradually adding more leaves.
3. When all the leaves are in the mortar, slice the garlic in half and discard the green sprout in the center (it imparts too sharp a flavor when eaten raw); add to the basil. Continue to pound until the mixture is quite smooth before you add oil or the oil will slosh around as you work the mixture.

continued

4. Add the oil very gradually while continuing to work the mixture to a silky smooth consistency. Stir in the cheeses and season with salt and pepper to taste. Set aside.
5. In a large pot, put the potatoes, 2 pinches of salt, and enough cold water to cover the potatoes by 2 inches. Bring to a boil and cook until the potatoes are tender when pierced with a paring knife, about 10 minutes. Drain and set aside.
6. Meanwhile, bring another pot of water to a boil. Stir in the pasta and cook until it's almost done, about 7½ minutes. Add the green beans and cook for 30 seconds. Reserving 1 cup of the liquid, drain the pasta and beans.
7. Gently toss the potatoes, pasta, and beans with the pesto, adding the reserved cooking water if needed to moisten. Season with salt and pepper, and serve hot or at room temperature.

How to Choose: For the smoothest pesto, look for basil with small, tender leaves. Occasionally, in early spring, growers bring their small-leaf Genovese or pesto basil plant starts to market. If you're a true pestophile, it's worth the extra effort to grow your own. Make sure the plant gets plenty of sun and be on guard for earwigs—they love nibbling on sweet young basil. Basil leaves are at their most pungent when small white flowers appear at the top of the plant. Don't be tempted to use the flowers and buds, though—they're rather bitter.

Grilled Tuna Steaks with Roasted Niçoise Salad

4 servings

When the weather is really warm and you can't imagine eating anything heavy, this version of niçoise salad is a great option. Instead of making the traditional cold salad of canned tuna and vegetables, I grill meaty tuna steaks and top them with roasted green beans, anchovies, and cherry tomatoes that melt into a chunky sauce. The basil sauce adds a sophisticated touch to this simple dish but is not essential.

FOR THE SALAD:

- Four 4-ounce tuna steaks, 1½ to 2 inches thick
- 2 tablespoons plus 1 teaspoon extra virgin olive oil, divided
- Salt and freshly ground black pepper
- 8 ounces green beans, stem ends trimmed
- ½ cup niçoise or other small black olives
- 1 pint cherry tomatoes
- 3 anchovy fillets
- 1 tablespoon balsamic vinegar

FOR THE OPTIONAL BASIL SAUCE:

- 1 medium garlic clove
- 1 tablespoon lemon juice
- 2 pinches kosher salt
- 2 cups basil leaves, loosely packed
- ¼ cup extra virgin olive oil

1. Preheat the oven to 400°F and line a rimmed baking sheet with parchment paper. Place the tuna on a large plate and rub with 1 teaspoon of the oil and a little salt and pepper. Allow the tuna to sit at room temperature while preparing the vegetables and sauce. (The fish will cook more evenly if it is at room temperature.)
2. Toss the green beans, olives, tomatoes, anchovies, vinegar, salt, pepper, and the remaining oil on the prepared baking sheet. Bake until the green beans are tender and the tomatoes begin to collapse, about 20 minutes.

continued

3. To make the basil sauce, halve the garlic lengthwise and remove the green sprout in the center. Grind the garlic with the lemon juice and salt in a mortar and pestle. Add the basil and work until the mixture is fairly smooth. Gradually add the oil and blend until the mixture is smooth and creamy. (Alternatively, make the pesto in a blender and add the oil while the machine is running.)
4. Preheat a grill or grill pan over high heat until very hot. (Flick a few drops of water on the grill; if the water sizzles and evaporates immediately, the grill is ready.) Carefully add the tuna and grill for 2 minutes. Turn over with a thin metal spatula and cook until the fish is medium rare, about 2 minutes longer.*
5. Place the tuna on 4 plates. Toss the vegetables together with tongs and place on the tuna, drizzle with the basil sauce, and serve.

* To test the doneness of fish, carefully insert a paring knife into the thickest part of the steak and hold it there for 3 seconds. Carefully touch the knife against your lower lip, sharp end angled away from you. If the knife is cold, the fish is still rare; if the knife is warm, the fish is medium; if the knife is hot, the fish is well done.

Chicken Chilaquiles with Tomatillo Sauce

6 servings

Chilaquiles are a traditional Mexican breakfast dish born of the frugal use of day-old corn tortillas layered with tomatillo sauce, cheese, and sometimes eggs. Gloria Martinez, a former coworker who hails from Mexico City, taught me to make this dish, though I've toned down the amount of chiles and added chicken to make it a dinner entrée.

1 pound tomatillos
1 Anaheim chile halved lengthwise, seeds and stem removed*
1 cup finely chopped onion
2 medium garlic cloves, unpeeled
2 tablespoons vegetable oil, divided
1½ teaspoons salt, divided
Freshly ground black pepper
3 split bone-in chicken breasts, skin removed
1 small garlic clove
1 bay leaf
¼ cup cilantro, roughly chopped
½ teaspoon dried oregano
2 teaspoons ground cumin
Six 6- to 8-inch corn tortillas
2 cups grated cheddar or Monterey Jack cheese
Sour cream, for garnish

1. Preheat the broiler and line a rimmed baking sheet with parchment paper. Toss the tomatillos, chile, onion, and garlic with 1 tablespoon of the oil on the prepared baking sheet. Sprinkle with ½ teaspoon of the salt and pepper, and broil, stirring once, until the tomatillos begin to collapse and brown, about 10 minutes. Scrape the mixture into a blender or food processor and allow to cool. Change the oven temperature to bake at 350°F.
2. Put the chicken in a small saucepan and add enough cold water to cover. Add the garlic, bay leaf, and 1 teaspoon of the salt and bring to a low simmer over medium-low heat. Cover and cook until the chicken registers 165°F on an instant-read thermometer or is no longer pink in the center, about 35 minutes. Drain, reserving 1 cup of the liquid. Roughly chop the chicken and set aside.

continued

3. Add the reserved liquid, cilantro, oregano, and cumin to the tomatillos in the blender and process until smooth. Season with salt and pepper and set aside.
4. Cut the tortillas into 1- by 2-inch strips. Toss them with the remaining oil and salt on a rimmed baking sheet. Bake until crisp, stirring once, about 20 minutes.
5. Sprinkle half the tortilla strips on the bottom of an 8- by 11½-inch baking dish. Distribute the chicken and half the tomatillo sauce over the strips and then cover with half the cheese. Repeat with the remaining strips, sauce, and cheese. Bake until the sauce is bubbly and the cheese is melted, about 40 minutes. Serve with the sour cream.

* Use care when handling any chile pepper: use gloves and never touch your eyes or mouth while working with them.

How to Choose: Tomatillos have a fruity, tart flavor that adds punch to cooked salsas, stews, and sauces. Choose firm tomatillos with bright green, yellow, or purple-striped skins and papery husks that cling tightly. Remove the sticky husks by soaking tomatillos in warm water for 10 minutes to loosen. Store tomatillos at room temperature for up to 4 days.

Marinated Chicken Skewers with Tomato Chutney

4 servings

This easy recipe for peak-of-season tomato chutney was given to me by Leena Ezekiel, a native of Assam, India, who runs A Taste of India Catering in Portland. The exotic flavor comes from a generous dose of *panch phoron*, a blend of equal parts whole cumin seed, nigella seed, fennel seed, fenugreek, and brown mustard seed. Panch phoron is available in Indian and some Asian markets, or you can make you own. (See Resources for good-quality spices.)

FOR THE CHICKEN SKEWERS:

1 tablespoon minced ginger
1 tablespoon minced garlic
1 teaspoon pure chile powder (not seasoning for chili con carne)
1 pinch salt
1 pound boneless, skinless chicken breasts
Bamboo skewers, soaked in cold water for several hours

FOR THE CHUTNEY:

1 tablespoon vegetable oil
1 teaspoon panch phoran
1 tablespoon minced ginger
1 pound Roma tomatoes, roughly chopped
½ cup sugar
1 teaspoon ground cumin
¼ to ½ teaspoon cayenne pepper
Salt
3 tablespoons chopped cilantro

1. Pound the ginger, garlic, chile powder, and salt in a small mortar and pestle to a fine paste, or vigorously chop the ingredients, smashing them against a cutting board with the side of a chef's knife. Cut the chicken into thin 3-inch strips and combine with the ginger paste in a sealable plastic bag. Marinate for at least 1 hour but preferably overnight.
2. To make the chutney, heat the oil in a large sauté pan over medium heat. Add the panch phoran and ginger, and stir until the spices start to pop. Add the tomatoes, cover, and cook over medium heat for 20 minutes, occasionally mashing the tomatoes with a potato masher.

▸ *continued*

3. Meanwhile, preheat a grill or broiler to high heat. Spray a rimmed baking sheet with non-stick cooking spray. Thread the chicken onto skewers without overcrowding and allow them stand at room temperature while finishing the chutney.
4. Stir the sugar, cumin, cayenne pepper, and salt into the tomatoes and continue to cook uncovered at a low simmer until the chutney is thickened and takes on a sheen, about 30 minutes. Remove from the heat and stir in the cilantro.
5. Broil or grill the skewers until cooked through, about 4 minutes per side. Serve immediately with individual bowls of chutney for dipping.

Roasted Chicken Peperonata

4 servings

Peperonata is an Italian bell pepper preparation that is usually served as an appetizer or side dish. I was introduced to peperonata as a sauce for roasted rabbit at a restaurant in Barbaresco, Italy, and was enraptured by the combination of sweet peppers, rosemary, and balsamic vinegar. Rabbit can be used instead of chicken; it will require about 5 minutes less baking time and should be nestled under the peperonata while baking.

3 tablespoons olive oil
1 cup chopped onion
1 red bell pepper, cut into thin strips
1 yellow bell pepper, cut into thin strips
One 3-inch sprig fresh rosemary
1 bay leaf
1 cup tomato puree or sauce
2 teaspoons sugar
1 tablespoon good-quality balsamic vinegar
8 bone-in chicken thighs
Salt and freshly ground black pepper
1 tablespoon vegetable oil

1. To make the peperonata, heat the oil in a large sauté pan over medium-high heat. Add the onion, peppers, rosemary, and bay leaf. Sauté slowly, stirring frequently, until the onion and peppers begin to brown, about 30 minutes. (Reduce the heat slightly if they begin to burn.) Add the tomato puree, sugar, and vinegar; cover and simmer over medium-low heat for 30 minutes. The mixture will be quite thick.
2. Preheat the oven to 350°F.
3. Rinse the chicken and pat dry with paper towels. Generously season it with salt and pepper on both sides. Heat the vegetable oil in a large sauté pan over medium-high heat. Carefully place the chicken, fat side down, in the pan. Sear until the skin is golden brown, about 3 minutes. Carefully turn the chicken over and cook for 3 minutes longer. (You may need to do this in batches.) Remove from the pan and pat dry with paper towels.
4. Put the peperonata in a large baking dish. Place the chicken on top and bake until the chicken is cooked through and an instant-read thermometer inserted in the thickest part of the thigh registers 165°F, about 35 minutes.
5. Allow the dish to rest at room temperature for 10 minutes. Remove the chicken from the pan and place on a large serving platter. Spoon off any fat floating on top of the peperonata. Spoon the peperonata over the chicken and serve with soft polenta or pasta.

Green Curry Chicken with Green Zebra Eggplant

4 servings

The small, squat green eggplant with white stripes, called Green Zebra, Kermit, or simply Thai eggplant, are often passed over at farmer's markets. I first encountered them while taking classes in Thailand and fell in love with their firm texture and mild flavor in curries and stir-frys. I was amazed to learn that Thais add raw Green Zebra eggplant to shredded green papaya salad, so mild is its flavor.

One 13.5-ounce can coconut milk
1 to 2 tablespoons Homemade Green Curry Paste (see recipe, page 90) or premade curry paste
3/4 pound boneless, skinless chicken thighs cut into bite-size pieces
12 ounces Green Zebra eggplant, stem end removed, quartered
1 red bell pepper, cut into 1/2-inch strips
1/2 cup thickly sliced shallots
6 kefir lime leaves*
2 teaspoons sugar
3 tablespoons fish sauce
1 cup loosely packed Thai basil**
1 lime, quartered

1. Spoon 2 tablespoons of the thick coconut cream from the top of the coconut milk into a wok or large sauté pan. Cook over medium-high heat for 1 minute. Reduce the heat to medium, turn on the kitchen fan or open windows (you must have ventilation when you fry curry paste), and add the curry paste; fry for 30 seconds, stirring constantly. Add the chicken and stir-fry until the chicken is opaque, 3 minutes.
2. Add the remaining coconut milk, eggplant, bell pepper, shallots, lime leaves, and sugar; stir well to combine. Bring to a simmer, cover, and cook until the eggplant is tender, about 30 minutes. Remove the lime leaves, stir in the fish sauce and basil, garnish with the lime, and serve with hot jasmine rice.

* Kefir lime leaves are tough, glossy green leaves of the kefir lime tree. They add a sprightly citrus flavor to curries and soups but are quite tough; warn your guests that they're not to be eaten. Find them at some farmer's markets or at Asian grocery stores. Freeze for up to 2 months in an airtight freezer bag.

** Thai basil is a purple-stemmed variety that has a distinctive anise-like flavor. Find it at farmer's markets and in most Asian grocery stores. European basil can be substituted.

Homemade Green Curry Paste

1½ cups

If you've never made curry paste, I encourage you to give it a try. Homemade curry paste is exponentially more fragrant than premade pastes, and it freezes well for up to 4 months.

2 tablespoons coriander seeds
2 teaspoons cumin seeds
10 black peppercorns
4 garlic cloves
16 green bird chiles, half seeded (see *, page 40)
2 tablespoons minced ginger
2 tablespoons minced fresh lemongrass (see instructions, page 40)
2 teaspoons lime zest
2 tablespoons fish sauce
2 teaspoons shrimp paste (optional)
1 cup cilantro, chopped

1. Heat a small sauté pan over medium heat. Dry-toast the coriander, cumin, and peppercorns until a few wisps of smoke rise from the pan, about 3 minutes. Immediately transfer them to a mortar and pestle or clean spice grinder and grind into a fine powder.
2. Put the garlic, bird chiles, ginger, lemongrass, and lime zest in a mortar and pestle, and grind into a fine paste. Add the fish sauce, shrimp paste, and cilantro and pound into a smooth paste. (Alternatively, combine all ingredients in a mini food processor or blender and process until smooth, adding a little water to get things moving if needed.) Store in an airtight container in the freezer for up to 4 months.

Flank Steak Fajitas with Interesting Peppers

8 servings

The hothouse bell peppers found in supermarkets lack the flavor and variety of peppers at farmer's markets from July to November. Ask vendors for sweet to moderately hot varieties and they will steer you in the right direction. My favorites included shiny red and yellow Corno di Toro "horn of the bull" peppers; tiny pimento peppers for fruity heat; long yellow-green Gypsy peppers for color and sweetness; and sweet, tangerine-colored Valencia peppers for smoky depth. If a pepper seems too hot for you, cut out the seeds *and* the pale veins before cooking. Always use care when handling peppers—wear gloves and refrain from touching your mouth or eyes.

1½ pounds flank or skirt steak
6 teaspoons vegetable oil, divided
1 tablespoon kosher salt
1 pound mixed mild to medium chile peppers, seeded and sliced into ½-inch strips
1 large onion, halved, peeled, and sliced from tip to root end
Juice of 1 lime
8 burrito-size flour tortillas
4 ounces pepper jack cheese, grated
Guacamole (optional)
Sour cream (optional)

1. Preheat the grill or a grill pan over high heat. If necessary cut the steak into 2 pieces to fit in the pan. Allow the steak to stand at room temperature for 30 minutes before cooking (it will cook more evenly if it starts at room temperature).
2. Rub the steak with 2 teaspoons of the oil and sprinkle the salt on both sides. Carefully lay the steak on the grill and sear for 3 minutes. Using tongs, carefully flip the meat over and cook until medium rare, about 3 minutes, depending on thickness, or until desired doneness.* Transfer to a plate and allow the steak to rest for 10 minutes.
3. Heat the remaining oil in a large cast iron skillet or heavy sauté pan over high heat. Add the peppers and onion without overcrowding; you may need to cook them in batches. Cook over high heat until they begin to brown, about 5 minutes. Pour them into a large serving bowl.
4. Transfer the steaks to a cutting board and slice against the grain and at a slight angle. Squeeze the lime juice over the slices and toss with the vegetables.

▸ *continued*

5. To assemble the fajitas, place a damp paper towel in the tortilla package to keep the tortillas pliable. Microwave them in the bag for 1 minute. (Alternatively, dampen a clean dish towel, remove the tortillas from their package, wrap them in the towel, and heat in a 200°F oven for 10 minutes.)
6. Serve the fajitas with bowls of the cheese, guacamole, and sour cream so guests can help themselves.

* The steak will continue to cook after you take it off of the heat. Flank steak turns shoe-leather tough if it is cooked more than medium, so you may want to err on the side of caution and pull it off the grill a little before you think it's done. You can always throw it back on the heat if it's too rare, but you can never make a steak less done.

Indian Spice–Stuffed Okra

8 appetizer servings

With this creative recipe, my friend and chef instructor Leena Ezekiel can convince anyone to love this much-maligned vegetable. There's no sliminess or odd texture to okra when it is prepared in this way, just tender little pods with a spicy kick that make a great appetizer for a cocktail party or barbecue. Pick young, small okra for the best results.

1 pound small okra
1 tablespoon ground coriander
1 tablespoon ground cumin
½ teaspoon pure chile powder (not seasoning blend for chili con carne)
1 tablespoon dry mango powder*
½ teaspoon salt
1½ teaspoons freshly ground black pepper
½ cup vegetable oil
1 cup thinly sliced red onion

1. Rinse the okra well, pat dry with paper towels, and trim away the tough stems. With a sharp paring knife, cut a slit in each okra but stop at least ¼ inch short of the end.
2. In a small bowl, mix the coriander, cumin, chile powder, mango powder, salt, and pepper. Using your thumb, open up the slit in the okra and stuff a generous pinch of the mixture into each one. Set aside.
3. Heat the oil in a large sauté pan over medium heat. Add the onion and sauté, stirring constantly, until it is golden brown, about 10 minutes.
4. Arrange the okra in a single layer in the sauté pan and reduce the heat to medium-low. Cook, turning occasionally, until the pods are light brown, about 20 minutes. Cover the pan and cook for 5 minutes, until okra are tender all the way through. Serve hot with Indian breads.

* Dried unripe mango powder, also called ***amchoor***, adds a slightly tart, savory taste to Indian food. Find it at Indian and Asian grocery stores, or order it from an online spice company that specializes in Indian spices. Substitute minced lime zest if you can't find amchoor.

Stuffed Vegetables Provençal

4 main course servings

Walk into any bistro in the south of France and the first thing you see is a table or bar set with an array of side dishes that accompany the à la carte menu. That's where I first tasted eggplant, summer squash, and tomatoes filled with bread crumbs, pancetta, and herbs. They've been a regular at my summer table ever since. They make an ideal vegetable keeper–clearing meal in late summer, and the filling is adaptable—add a local artisan cheese, browned ground lamb, or torn Swiss chard to make the recipe yours.

2 small (12 to 16 ounces) eggplant
6 teaspoons extra virgin olive oil, divided
2 medium summer squash (zucchini, pattypan, or yellow crookneck)
2 small bell peppers
4 medium tomatoes
2 ounces pancetta or bacon, coarsely chopped
½ cup finely minced onion
1 teaspoon minced garlic
1 teaspoon dried *herbes de Provence**
2 cups fresh bread crumbs**
2 tablespoons chopped Italian parsley
¼ cup grated Parmesan cheese
Salt and freshly ground black pepper

1. Preheat the oven to 350°F and line a baking sheet with parchment paper. Halve each eggplant lengthwise and scoop out the pulp with a melon baller or small spoon, leaving a ½-inch border around the edge and bottom. Finely chop the pulp and set aside.
2. Put the eggplant shells on the prepared baking sheet and brush them with 2 teaspoons of the oil. Bake until they are just tender when pierced with a paring knife, about 20 minutes. Remove from the oven and set aside.
3. Halve the squash and bell peppers lengthwise. Remove the seeds from the peppers. Carefully scoop out the pulp in the center of the squash to make a shell, finely chop the pulp, and set aside.
4. Slice off the top quarter of each tomato; scoop out the seeds and discard. Remove the flesh from each center and chop it roughly with the edible portions of the tomato tops; set aside. Place the squash and tomato shells on the baking sheet with the eggplant shells.

5. Heat the remaining oil in a large sauté pan over medium-high heat. Cook the pancetta until crisp. Add the onion, chopped eggplant, garlic, and herbes de Provence, and then sauté until the eggplant is tender, about 5 minutes. Add the chopped squash and tomatoes; continue to cook for 10 minutes, stirring occasionally. Put the mixture in a large bowl.
6. Add the bread crumbs, parsley, and Parmesan to the vegetable mixture and stir to combine. Add salt and pepper to taste. Mound the bread crumb filling into the vegetable shells and bake until tender but before the tomatoes collapse, 30 to 40 minutes. Serve hot or at room temperature.

* Herbes de Provence is an herb blend that commonly contains basil, fennel seed, lavender, marjoram, rosemary, and thyme. It is used to season chicken, meat, and stuffings. Find it at grocery stores and online (see Resources).

** To make fresh bread crumbs, allow slices of bread to sit out overnight or toast them briefly in a 200°F oven for 30 minutes. Tear into pieces and pulse in a food processor (or chop finely with a chef's knife) to create fine, moist crumbs. Make extra crumbs and freeze some for future use. They always come in handy for vegetable casseroles, macaroni and cheese, and as a thickener for soups.

How to Choose: Look for smooth, shiny eggplant with taut skin and no wrinkles. Pass up eggplant with soft brown areas, which are usually bitter because of cold damage. Don't refrigerate them; use them for a still-life display and cook within a few days.

For eggplant with a mild flavor and creamy flesh, try the small, elongated Asian varieties (like the lavender-skinned Machiaw) or dark purple "Indian" eggplants. For eggplant that holds its shape in sautés and sauces, try the purple- or lavender-striped varieties like Listada de Gandia or Rosa Bianca. The only time it's necessary to salt eggplant is when frying it; salting keeps the slices from absorbing too much oil and has little effect on whether the eggplant is bitter. Choose a fresh eggplant grown with care, and bitterness shouldn't plague you.

Fig Preserves for Glazed Ham

Six 1-pint jars

Fig trees bear fruit twice a year—a small fruiting in the spring and a more vigorous, flavorful round in late summer or early fall. This jam is a good spread for English muffins and the like, but I make it specifically for its ability to turn bone-in ham into a glazed delicacy. Mix 1 cup of fig preserves with ½ cup Dijon mustard; smother the ham with the mixture before roasting. The jam caramelizes and creates a sweet dark glaze that is highly addictive. If canning seems too much of a chore, freeze the jam for up to 3 months.

4¾ cups water, divided
5 pounds fresh figs
4 cups sugar
1 tablespoon chopped ginger
Zest and juice of 1 orange

1. Bring 4 cups of the water to a boil in a large pot. Add the figs and remove the pot from the heat; allow to sit for 30 minutes.
2. Remove the figs with a slotted spoon. Discard the fig stems, halve the figs, and place them in a large saucepan with the remaining water, sugar, and ginger. Bring to a rolling boil. Reduce the heat to maintain a gentle simmer, stir frequently, and cook until the figs break up and the mixture is a jam-like consistency, about 30 minutes. Mash large pieces that remain with a potato masher or pass through a food mill. Stir in the orange zest and juice.
3. Meanwhile, prepare the jars for canning (see instructions, page 108). Pour the hot jam into the prepared jars, seal the lids, transfer to a canning rack, and submerge in boiling water for 10 minutes. Remove from the water and allow the jars to sit at room temperature overnight. Discard any jars that do not seal. (Alternatively, pack preserves into freezer-safe containers, allow to cool, seal with lids, and freeze for up to 3 months.)

Peach and Blackberry Hazelnut Crisp

8 servings

Peaches and blackberries are natural flavor partners; fortunately they come into season at the same time (late summer). If you like fruit crisps especially juicy, reduce the flour in the fruit mixture to just a few tablespoons. I leave the skins on the peaches because they add fiber and flavor; they can be peeled if you prefer.

FOR THE HAZELNUT TOPPING:

3 tablespoons all-purpose flour
3 tablespoons firmly packed brown sugar
4 teaspoons granulated sugar
¼ teaspoon ground cinnamon
⅛ teaspoon ground nutmeg
1 pinch salt
3 tablespoons cold unsalted butter, cut into ¼-inch pieces
⅓ cup old fashioned rolled oats
½ cup hazelnuts, toasted, skinned, and chopped (see instructions, page 146)

FOR THE FRUIT:

1 pound ripe peaches, pitted and sliced
1¼ pounds (3 cups) blackberries or marionberries
1 teaspoon lemon juice
½ teaspoon lemon zest
⅓ cup all-purpose flour
3 tablespoons granulated sugar
Vanilla ice cream or frozen yogurt (optional)

1. Preheat the oven to 350°F. Lightly spray a 2-quart baking dish with nonstick cooking spray.
2. To make the hazelnut topping, in a food processor or large bowl combine the flour, sugars, cinnamon, nutmeg, and salt. Add the butter pieces and pulse until they are the size of small peas. (Alternatively, blend with a pastry blender or your fingers.) Add the oats and hazelnuts, and refrigerate.

continued

3. To prepare the fruit, toss the peaches, berries, lemon juice, lemon zest, flour, and sugar in a large bowl. Pour into the prepared baking dish and sprinkle hazelnut topping evenly over the top.
4. Place the baking dish on a baking sheet and bake until the fruit is bubbly and the topping is golden, 45 minutes to 1 hour. Cool 30 minutes and serve with the ice cream.

How to Choose: Peaches are normally picked before they are fully ripe. Look for peaches that have a cream or yellow background with no sign of bruising or green around the stem. The red blush is not a sign of a ripe peach. Instead, use your nose: smell peaches at their "belly button"; they should smell sweet and make you want to chomp into them. To ripen peaches quickly, store them at room temperature in a brown paper bag. Eat them as soon as they become fragrant and yield to a little pressure when pressed at the seam side. Refrigerate ripe peaches for up to 2 days in a plastic bag. Peaches, like strawberries, are a heavily sprayed crop—it's a good idea to choose organic when available.

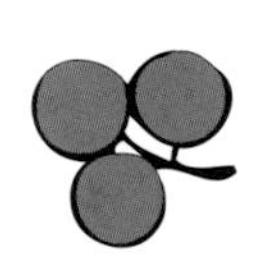

Raspberry Truffle Cake

6 to 8 servings

There's really nothing better than raspberries paired with good-quality bittersweet chocolate. This creamy mousse cake—adapted from a recipe by Melissa Lehmkuhl, pastry chef at ROUX—has an ultra-decadent texture thanks to a brief baking time in a water bath and then 8 hours of chilling to allow it to set. The result is a rich, velvety confection studded with sweet-tart raspberries that melts in your mouth. Serve the cake with freshly whipped cream and more raspberries.

12 ounces bittersweet chocolate, chopped
10 tablespoons unsalted butter, cut into small pieces
5 eggs, at room temperature
¼ teaspoon kosher salt
¼ teaspoon vanilla extract
⅛ teaspoon almond extract (optional)
½ pint raspberries, divided
Hot water, for baking
Whipped cream, for garnish

1. Preheat the oven to 375°F. Spray a 9-inch springform pan with nonstick cooking spray. Tightly wrap the outside of the pan with 2 layers of foil.
2. Place a large metal bowl over a pan of barely simmering water, add the chocolate and butter, and stir until the mixture is smooth. Remove the bowl from the pan and allow the mixture to cool to room temperature.
3. Meanwhile, whip the eggs, salt, vanilla, and almond extract in an electric mixer on high speed until pale yellow and tripled in volume, about 10 minutes. Fold half the mixture into the chocolate mixture until no egg streaks remain. Gently fold in the remaining egg mixture (do not overmix or the batter will deflate). Pour the batter into the prepared springform pan.

4. Set aside ½ cup of the raspberries for garnish and sprinkle the remaining raspberries evenly over the batter. Push them into the batter until they are almost submerged.
5. Place the pan in a large baking dish and transfer to the oven. Carefully pour enough hot water into the baking dish to come halfway up the cake pan. Bake until the top is no longer glossy and the cake pulls away from the side when the pan is tilted slightly, 15 to 20 minutes. (*Do not overbake.* The cake will still be very soft but will become firmer when refrigerated.) Remove the cake pan from the water and allow it to sit at room temperature until cool. Cover the pan with plastic wrap and refrigerate for *at least* 8 hours before serving. *If you omit this step, the cake will fall apart.*
6. To unmold, dip the bottom of the pan in a bowl of very hot water for 15 seconds and run a thin knife around the edge of the cake to loosen. Release the springform and shake gently to release the cake. Serve with the whipped cream and remaining raspberries.

Fresh Cherry Muffins

12 muffins

Pastry Chef Lee Posey of Pearl Bakery in Portland uses fresh Bing cherries (available from mid-June to as late as August) for this recipe, but says the batter has many options. "Huckleberries would be great, as would blueberries. In winter I make them with dried cranberries and a little orange zest."

6 tablespoons unsalted butter, at room temperature
3/4 cup sugar
1/2 teaspoon salt
1 egg
1 teaspoon almond extract
2 1/2 cups all-purpose flour
2 teaspoons baking powder
1/3 teaspoon baking soda
1 cup whole milk
8 ounces fresh Bing cherries, pitted* and roughly chopped
1/2 cup sliced almonds, toasted
1/4 cup sliced almonds, raw

1. Preheat the oven to 375°F. Spray 2 muffin tins with nonstick cooking spray or line them with paper muffin cups. Beat the butter, sugar, and salt in a mixing bowl until light and fluffy. Scrape down the sides with a rubber spatula. Add the egg and almond extract; beat to combine.
2. Whisk the flour, baking powder, and baking soda in a medium bowl until well combined. With a wooden spoon, add to butter mixture in two additions, alternating with the milk. Mix until the ingredients are just incorporated; do not overmix.
3. Stir in the cherries and toasted almonds. Use a small ice cream scoop to divide the batter among the muffin cups. Sprinkle the tops with the raw almonds and bake until golden brown and a wooden skewer inserted into the center comes out clean, 20 to 25 minutes.
4. Transfer to a cooling rack and cool for 30 minutes in the tins. Remove muffins from tins and serve. Muffins will keep well for up to 2 days or frozen for up to 3 weeks.

* To pit cherries, squeeze each cherry inside a plastic bag until the pits are dislodged; the bag acts as a shield to keep the juice from staining your clothes and cutting board.

Spice-Poached Peaches with Lavender Syrup and Mascarpone Whip

4 servings

Chef Ande Janousek of Carmelita serves this fruit-centered dessert with lemon pistachio biscotti; you can pick up the cookies at your favorite vendor instead. About the time peaches are in season, bundles of fresh lavender are being sold. Here, Chef Janousek uses the delicate flavor of lavender flowers to make a sugar syrup to garnish the dish. The poaching liquid can be reserved and used later to poach other summer goodies like apricots, berries, and nectarines.

FOR THE LAVENDER SYRUP:

½ cup granulated sugar
¼ cup water
½ teaspoon lavender flowers

FOR THE PEACHES:

2 cups water
2 cups dry white wine
1 cup granulated sugar
1 cinnamon stick
1 bay leaf
1 teaspoon whole cloves
1 teaspoon black peppercorns
1 star anise
Zest of ½ lemon
1 pinch salt
2 large peaches, peeled

FOR THE MASCARPONE WHIP:

1 cup mascarpone cheese, at room temperature
1 teaspoon milk
2 tablespoons powdered sugar
¼ vanilla bean

1. In a small saucepan, heat the sugar, water, and lavender over medium heat, stirring occasionally, until the sugar is dissolved. Set aside to cool.
2. To prepare the peaches, combine the water, wine, sugar, cinnamon stick, bay leaf, cloves, peppercorns, anise, lemon zest, and salt in a saucepan just large enough to hold the peaches snugly. Bring the mixture to a simmer, add the peaches, and simmer gently for 10 to 15 minutes, turning the fruit occasionally. Remove the peaches, halve them lengthwise, and discard the pits. Put each half in a separate bowl, cut side up.
3. For the mascarpone whip, combine the cheese, milk, and powdered sugar in a small mixing bowl. Split the vanilla bean with the tip of a paring knife, scrape out the sticky black seeds, add to the cheese mixture, and whip until fluffy.
4. Mound one-quarter of the cheese mixture in the center of each peach. Drizzle with the lavender syrup and serve with biscotti.

White Peach and Vanilla Jam

6 pints

When white peaches come into season, their sweet aroma can stop me in my tracks in the middle of the market. They have a more delicate flavor than their more acidic yellow cousins that marries well with vanilla, as in this recipe for homemade jam. White peaches break down quite a bit while cooking; for this recipe I buy about a quarter of the peaches in the not-quite-ripe state so the jam will have chunks of fruit in it.

If you're new to canning, go to www.homecanning.com for instructional videos and safety tips. I'm sure you'll find canning to be simple and well worth the effort. Imagine how appreciative you'll feel in the middle of February when you sit down to a breakfast of toast and aromatic peach jam that tastes like summer itself.

6 pounds white peaches
2 tablespoons fresh lemon juice
5 cups sugar
1 vanilla bean

1. To sterilize the jars, run them through the dishwasher on the rinse cycle just before starting to make the jam. Keep the jars warm in the dishwasher until you're ready to fill them. (Alternatively, you can sterilize the jars with very hot—not boiling—water and keep them warm until ready to fill.) Place the lids and collars in a small saucepan and heat over medium-low heat until hot, but do not boil as excessive heat will damage the rubber adhesive on the lids.
2. Peel the peaches using a sharp serrated peeler like the Messermeister swivel peeler (see Resources). Halve the peaches, remove the pits, and slice the peaches into ½-inch-thick wedges. Combine the peaches, any peach juice that has accumulated, and the lemon juice in a large, heavy-bottomed pot. Bring to a simmer.
3. Halve the vanilla bean lengthwise, use the blunt end of a paring knife to scrape out the sticky black seeds, and add the seeds and bean to the pot. Stir in the sugar and bring to a boil over medium-high heat. Stir occasionally and cook until the mixture reaches 220°F on a candy thermometer. Skim off any foam that surfaces. While the jam is cooking, fill a large stockpot of water to within 4 inches from the top. Bring to a boil.

4. Quickly ladle the jam into the warm jars, allowing ¼ inch of space at the top. With a moist paper towel, wipe away any spills from the rims and threaded sides of the jars. Center the hot lids on the jars and screw on the bands until just fingertip tight; don't crank them closed.
5. Carefully place the jars in a canning rack (see Resources) and slowly lower it into the boiling water. Be sure the water covers the jars by at least 2 inches. Increase the heat to medium-high and bring to a gentle boil. Set a timer for 10 minutes, adjusting for altitude.* Put kitchen towels on the counter.
6. At the end of 10 minutes, turn off the heat; carefully remove the jars and put them on the towels. Let them sit for 30 minutes. You'll hear a satisfying "thup" coming from each lid as it forms a vacuum seal. Test the seals by gently pushing down on the lids. If a lid flexes, the seal was not made and the jam should be refrigerated and used within 1 week, or frozen in a plastic airtight container and used within 3 months. Remove the bands from the jars and gently pick up the jars up by their lids to test again for a good seal. Store the jars in a cool, dark place.

* You must adjust the canning time depending on your altitude. Refer to the chart at www.homecanning.com, or the instructions that came with your canning jars, for times.

FALL

WE SWITCH FROM T-SHIRTS AND SHORTS TO SWEATERS AND JEANS, the air finally gets a little crisper, and leaves crunch underfoot while we stroll through the market. After the heat of late summer, nothing feels better than spending quality time getting reacquainted with our heavy kitchen pots and the earthy flavors of fall. We start thinking about turning on the oven again—for roasted squash, duck breast, and root vegetables. It's also time for the earthy taste of amber chanterelles, plump porcini, and meaty lobster mushrooms—it seems as if each week there's a new mushroom to work with. It's time to start baking again, if only to fill the house with the aroma of cinnamon and apples, golden bread, or roasting pears. We all settle in and nest now to ready ourselves for the limited light and cold blustery weather to come while still getting the bounty that comes at the end of the harvest.

meet the producer

It's October 1 and Barb Foulke is up before dawn with her husband, Fritz; sons, Evan and Toby; and daughter, Jocie. They're rushing to get their sixty-acre hazelnut orchard ready for what will be the longest day of their year. The recent hot days and cool nights cause the hazelnuts on their seven thousand trees to swell, contract, and drop from the branches. The Foulkes must hustle to collect them before the hard rains of autumn begin.

Barb rakes the periphery of the orchard; Toby handles the sweeper—a huge piece of machinery that blows the nuts, fallen leaves, and debris into a neat pile in the center of each row. Fritz follows on a tractor pulling a harvester that vacuums up the nuts while it blows debris out the other end. Barb's uncle, Ray, and father, Gene, drive forklifts to and fro, carrying 1,100-pound wooden totes full of nuts to the barn where the nuts will be sorted and held in dry storage in their shells for up to a year. They will work into the night, switching on the tractor headlights, until every nut is collected.

Barb and Fritz bought their orchard in 1998 as a sort of hobby while they kept their day jobs as a nurse practitioner and a doctor, respectively. For the first few years, the Foulkes sold their harvest to middlemen for a standard commodity price. It was frustrating for Barb: "They drive in, grab your product, and the price they get for the nuts doubles within five days and then doubles again. Every time the price doubles, the quality had dropped in increments of about the same," she explains.

The Foulkes sold exclusively to the commodities market for four years while they focused their energies on repairing farm equipment, pruning efficiently, and establishing a healthy orchard by replacing trees with a disease-resistant hazelnut variety.

In 2001, after their best harvest to date, the bottom of the market dropped out, and the contracted buyers told the Foulkes they would receive a very low price for their harvest. "That was the last straw," Barb recalls. "I grew up with my father accepting commodity prices and grumbling about it.

So when they sent me a letter telling me my nuts were only worth thirty cents a pound, I thought, 'I cannot allow those people to come in and ruin my product and get six times the price.'"

So she decided to try to sell her hazelnuts directly, a fairly unusual idea for a farm that was more of a hobby than a full-time career. Barb and her daughter designed a Web site, and Freddy Guys Hazelnuts was born. Though Barb was doing a brisk mail-order business, she couldn't sell all of the 150,000 pounds of hazelnuts her orchard yielded annually.

"A friend suggested vending at a farmer's market. So I went to the Beaverton farmer's market, and I could sell a couple hundred dollars of nuts in one day! And then chefs started asking if I'd deliver. The markets have been the most important aspect of my success. Without them I would have quit."

Barb's interaction with her customers at Portland-area farmer's markets has helped her spawn new ideas beyond simple shelled nuts. She now sells a unique line of hazelnut products, from heavenly chocolate hazelnut spread to hazelnut pizza dough, all made in a small, squeaky-clean production kitchen next to her shelling barn.

After a very long, dusty day of harvesting, I sit with Barb and Fritz on an overstuffed couch in their comfortable home just steps from the orchard. Does she ever get tired of all the work? "Are you kidding?" she grins as she winks at her husband. "This is mental therapy for me! As I get more successful, it pushes me forward. I've always been responsible as can be while I make money for someone else. This is *my* project, *my* orchard, and *my* little business. I think it's those two letters M-Y that dictate that Freddy Guys is going be the highest quality it can possibly be. Besides, I can come home after my day job and get on a tractor and mow and sing at the top of my lungs! It just feels really good to be out there on the land."

Mostarda D'Uva with Artisan Cheese

1½ cups

This sweet-savory chutney from the north of Italy is made to use overripe grapes left over after the wine-pressing season. The dark jam, called *cugnà* in northwestern Italian dialect, is served with fresh cheese and crusty bread, or even as a chutney for roasts.

Chef Johnathan Sundstrom was kind enough to share his recipe for the spread, which he features on his cheese menu at Lark, his James Beard Award–winning Seattle restaurant.

1 pound seedless Concord or red wine grapes, stems removed
½ pound apples, pears, or quince (or combination), peeled and roughly chopped
½ pound sugar or cinderella pumpkin, peeled and chopped
¼ cup sugar, plus additional as needed
1 cinnamon stick
½ teaspoon balsamic or red wine vinegar (optional)
1 cup hazelnuts, toasted, skinned, and chopped (see instructions, page 146)
1 cup walnuts, toasted and roughly chopped
4 to 6 ounces artisan cheese such as Sally Jackson goat or manchego

1. Combine the grapes, apples, pumpkin, sugar, and cinnamon stick in a large, heavy-bottomed pan over medium heat. Cover and cook, stirring occasionally, until the fruit begins to release some of its juice, about 5 minutes.
2. Uncover the pan, reduce the heat to very low, and cook until the mixture is a thick, jam-like consistency, 3 to 4 hours. Stir and mash the grapes with the back of a spoon occasionally. Be sure the mixture is not scorching; add a few tablespoons of water if the mixture begins to burn.
3. Taste and then add more sugar or honey to sweeten to your preference. If the mixture is too sweet, add the vinegar. Stir in the nuts and cook for 30 minutes. Transfer the mixture to a serving bowl and allow it to cool to room temperature before serving with the cheese. Refrigerate any remaining jam in an airtight container for up to 2 weeks.

How to Choose: Traditional mostarda d'uva is made with Sangiovese wine grapes, but Concord or black seedless grapes work well too. Look for grapes that show no signs of shriveling and still sport a dusty-white blush to them, a sign the grapes have been handled carefully. Refrigerate the grapes in a perforated plastic bag, and allow them to come almost to room temperature before eating out of hand.

Orchard Salad with Sweet Curry Dressing

4 servings

The mild spiciness of fresh curry powder in the dressing counters the sweetness of apples and balsamic-plumped currants in this autumnal salad. Most folks have stale curry powder lurking in the back of the spice drawer. Dispose of it—it's not helping anyone. For this recipe you need fresh, top-quality curry powder to make the dressing sing. I recommend Penzeys Spices sweet curry blend (see Resources). If you are prepping the salad in advance, use Braeburn apples; their firm texture and resistance to browning will make a prettier salad.

½ cup dried currants
Good-quality balsamic vinegar for soaking
1 small (about 1 cup) Granny Smith or other sweet-tart apple, peeled, cored, and roughly chopped
2 tablespoons fresh lemon juice
1 tablepoon apple cider vinegar
1 small garlic clove, green center removed
1 teaspoon chopped ginger
1½ teaspoons good-quality curry powder
1 teaspoon salt
1 teaspoon honey
¼ cup vegetable oil
¼ cup extra virgin olive oil
Salt and freshly ground black pepper
5 cups torn romaine or green leaf lettuce
1 medium Braeburn or Honeycrisp apple, cored and sliced into ½-inch-thick wedges
½ cup almonds, toasted and roughly chopped

1. In a small airtight container, combine the currants and enough balsamic vinegar to cover them. Soak for at least 1 hour before using.
2. To make the dressing, combine the apple, lemon juice, apple cider vinegar, garlic, ginger, curry powder, salt, and honey in a blender; process until smooth. With the machine running, slowly add the vegetable oil and then olive oil. Season to taste with salt and pepper.
3. In a large bowl, combine 2 tablespoons of the currants (drained), lettuce, sliced apple, and almonds. Add enough dressing to lightly coat the lettuce, divide among salad plates, and serve. You will have extra dressing; refrigerate in an airtight container for several weeks. The remaining currants can be kept in balsamic vinegar in the refrigerator indefinitely.

Warm Chèvre, Radicchio, and Forelle Pear Salad with Candied Walnuts

4 servings

Goat cheese, or chèvre, is becoming a mainstream product in the United States. At the markets it's common to see more than one artisan cheese maker selling handmade cheeses made with milk from their animals. The hard work and artistry involved in cheese making is intricately connected to the land, much like growing vegetables. The flavor of a cheese is dependent on what the animals graze on; a diet of sweet clover makes a sweet, grassy cheese, for example. Next time you see cheese makers at your market, stop and sample their art.

2 tablespoons butter, divided
2 ounces walnuts
2 tablespoons brown sugar
2 tablespoons brandy
1 tablespoon balsamic vinegar
½ teaspoon Dijon mustard
¼ teaspoon minced shallots
3 tablespoons extra virgin olive oil
2 ounces seasonal baby greens
½ head radicchio, cored and thinly sliced
3 Forelle pears, cored and thinly sliced
4 ounces chèvre cut into 8 discs*
¼ cup rice flour**

1. To make the candied walnuts, line a dinner plate with parchment paper or foil. Heat 1 tablespoon of the butter in a large sauté pan over medium-high heat. Add the walnuts and brown sugar; cook, stirring constantly, until the sugar begins to melt. Keep the pan cover handy. Reduce the heat and carefully add the brandy to the pan. The fumes will ignite. Cover the pan if the flames leap too high. (If you are using an electric stove, you may need to ignite the brandy with a kitchen match.) Shake the pan; when the flames subside, pour the nuts onto the prepared plate and allow to cool.
2. To make the salad, whisk the vinegar, mustard, and shallots. Add the oil in a slow stream, whisking constantly. In a large bowl, toss the greens, radicchio, and pears with the dressing; divide among 4 salad plates.

3. Coat the chèvre evenly with the flour. Heat the remaining butter in a small sauté pan over medium-high heat. Add the chèvre and quickly fry until golden brown, about 30 seconds per side.
4. Place the chèvre on top of the salads, sprinkle with the walnuts, and serve.

* Slicing chèvre can be tricky. Use a knife specifically for soft cheese, or hold a length of clean dental floss taut and saw the chèvre into rounds.

** Rice flour can be found at health food stores and some grocery stores. To make your own, grind raw white rice to a fine powder in a clean coffee or spice grinder.

How to Choose: Radicchio, a leafy member of the chicory family, comes in several forms and is best in fall through early spring. The most common variety is the grapefruit-size Chioggia, with white and burgundy leaves. Other varieties include the less bitter yellow Castelfranco and the elongated burgundy Treviso. Whichever variety you choose, look for heavy heads with crisp leaves and no browning on the tips of the outside leaves.

Though radicchio is normally served raw in salads in the United States, in Italy it is commonly served braised or grilled. Try cutting it into quarters and braising in a bit of bacon fat and balsamic vinegar; you'll never look at radicchio the same way again.

Roasted Butternut Soup in Dumpling Squash Bowls

6 servings

There are dozens of winter squash varieties; all are variable in both flavor and texture. I've found that butternut has the most reliable flavor, with cheese pumpkin and Jarrahdale a close second and third. I bake small dumpling squash for this recipe and use them as edible soup bowls, offering guests the flavors of two squash in one meal. If time is short, skip this step and serve the soup in warm bowls.

3 pounds butternut squash
1 teaspoon salt
2 garlic cloves
6 black peppercorns
1 teaspoon coriander seeds
½ teaspoon fennel seeds
1 tablespoon olive oil
6 small Sweet Dumpling squash, about 1 pound each (optional)
1 tablespoon butter
1 cup chopped onion
2 carrots, peeled and chopped
3 to 4 cups chicken or vegetable stock
1 bay leaf
Salt and freshly ground black pepper
Ground nutmeg
½ cup hazelnuts, toasted, skinned, and chopped (see instructions, page 146), for garnish
3 green onions, chopped, for garnish

1. Preheat the oven to 350°F and line a baking sheet with parchment paper. Halve the butternut squash lengthwise: insert a chef's knife through the center of the bulb-shaped end and cut through it, rotating the squash and cutting through the slender neck end to split it. Scrape out the seeds and stringy bits.
2. Pound the salt, garlic, peppercorns, coriander seeds, and fennel seeds in a mortar and pestle until they resemble a coarse paste. (Alternatively, crush the spices with the bottom of a large sauté pan and combine with finely chopped garlic.) Add the oil and rub the mixture on the squash halves. Place the halves cut side down on the prepared sheet, and bake until they are tender when pierced with a fork, about 1 hour.

continued

3. Meanwhile, prepare the squash bowls. Prick the tops of each Sweet Dumpling squash with a paring knife. Microwave for 1 minute. Hold 1 squash on its side and cut off the top. Scoop out the seeds and stringy bits and place the squash cut side up in a lightly oiled dish. Repeat with the remaining Sweet Dumpling squash. Pour ½ inch of water in the bottom of the dish and bake until the squash are tender when pierced with a fork, 40 minutes to 1 hour. Keep warm until ready to serve.
4. In a large soup pot, heat the butter over medium heat. Add the onion and carrots and cook until the onion begins to brown, about 10 minutes.
5. Use a soup spoon to scrape the butternut flesh away from the skin and add it to the pot. Stir in the stock and bay leaf and simmer for 30 minutes.
6. Remove the bay leaf. In a blender, with the lid slightly ajar to allow steam to escape, puree the soup in batches. Return the soup to the pot and reheat until it is hot. Season with salt, pepper, and nutmeg to taste.
7. Fill each squash bowl with the soup, sprinkle with hazelnuts and green onions, and serve.

How to Choose: Pick butternut squash that has no trace of green showing beneath the beige skin around the stem. The deeper gold the skin, the richer the flavor. The highest flesh yield is in the neck portion, so pick squash that have long, thick necks. Butternut squash can be kept at room temperature for weeks provided there are no nicks in the skin and the stem is still attached. Pick Sweet Dumpling squash that stand upright without wobbling and feel heavy for their size.

Whole Wheat Penne with Wild Mushrooms

4 servings

This recipe was developed for classes I taught on healthy cooking for cancer prevention with a group of Providence Medical Center physicians. It was a great way to introduce wild mushrooms and whole grain pasta into students' diets. Not every sauce can stand up to the flavor of whole wheat pasta, but the earthiness of wild mushrooms, creamy roasted garlic, and fresh herbs are bold enough to do the job. Try porcini, chanterelles, black trumpet, or oyster mushrooms; whatever foragers offer at the farmer's market will work.

1 head garlic
3 tablespoons olive oil, divided
Salt and freshly ground black pepper
¼ cup warm water
½ cup finely chopped onion
8 ounces wild mushrooms, cleaned and sliced
2 tablespoons chopped fresh herbs (rosemary, parsley, thyme, sage)
1 pinch red chili flakes
2 cups chicken or mushroom broth
Juice of ½ lemon
12 ounces whole wheat penne pasta
½ cup grated Parmesan cheese
2 tablespoons butter

1. Preheat the oven to 350°F. Use a serrated knife to cut the top quarter off the garlic. Place the remainder in a small ramekin, drizzle with 1 teaspoon of the oil, sprinkle with salt and pepper, and cover with foil. Bake for 45 minutes, or until the garlic squishes easily when gently squeezed. Remove from the oven, add the water, cover with the foil, and allow to sit for 30 minutes. Squeeze the sides to release the cloves from their papery skins; discard the skins. Mash cloves into the ramekin with the soaking water.
2. Heat the remaining oil in a large sauté pan over medium-high heat. Add the onion and sauté until it is soft and beginning to brown, about 8 minutes. Add the firmest mushrooms to the pan and sauté for 2 minutes. Stir in the fresh herbs, chili flakes, and remaining mushrooms; sauté until the mushrooms begin to brown and become tender.

continued

3. Deglaze the pan with the broth and lemon juice, scraping up any browned bits on the bottom of the pan. Add the garlic and gently simmer over low heat.
4. Bring a large pot of salted water to a boil. Add the pasta and cook until al dente, 8 to 10 minutes. (Whole wheat pasta usually takes longer to cook than white wheat pasta.) Reserving 1 cup of the cooking liquid, drain the pasta.
5. Put the pasta in a large serving bowl, and toss with the mushroom sauce, cheese, and butter. Stir in the reserved liquid if the pasta seems too dry. Season with salt and pepper and serve.

Herb-Crusted Tofu with Marsala Mushroom Gravy and Garlic Mashed Potatoes

4 servings

Fearn Smith and Guy Weigold are so dedicated to keeping a connection with the land that they named their restaurant The Farm Café. Almost everything on the menu is locally sourced, including this dish using tofu made a block away at Ota Tofu Company. This comfy entrée with rich mushroom gravy is a mainstay on their menu and is popular with vegetarians and omnivores alike.

FOR THE TOFU:

16 ounces firm tofu
1 cup soy sauce
1 cup dry Marsala wine
1 cup water
1 cup fresh bread crumbs
1 cup Panko breading*
2 teaspoons kosher salt
2 teaspoons freshly ground black pepper
2 tablespoons fresh thyme leaves, stems removed, chopped
2 tablespoons vegetable oil

FOR THE MASHED POTATOES:

6 garlic cloves, unpeeled
2 tablespoons extra virgin olive oil
1½ pounds (2 large) russet potatoes
1 tablespoon kosher salt
2 teaspoons fresh rosemary leaves, finely chopped
½ cup sour cream or vegan soy cream
Freshly ground black pepper

FOR THE MUSHROOM GRAVY:

2 tablespoons olive oil
1 cup chopped onion
2 cups wild or cultivated mushrooms, sliced
1 cup dry Marsala wine
1 teaspoon *herbs de Provence*
¾ cup sour cream or vegan soy cream
Salt and freshly ground black pepper

1. Place the tofu between two plates with a few heavy cans on top to press out excess moisture. Allow to sit for 30 minutes; pat dry with paper towels. Slice into 4 equal slabs; cut each slab diagonally to make two triangular pieces.
2. Put the soy sauce, wine, and water in a shallow baking dish. Submerge the tofu in the marinade for at least 1 hour at room temperature or up to 8 hours refrigerated.
3. Preheat the oven to 200°F. While the tofu is marinating, make the mashed potatoes. Put the garlic and olive oil in a small baking dish (a custard cup works well), cover with foil, and bake until tender, about 20 minutes.
4. Place unpeeled potatoes in a large pot of cold water, add salt, and bring to a boil. Cook until the potatoes are tender when pierced with a paring knife, about 45 minutes. Drain, cool slightly, and slip the skins off with your fingers; return potatoes to the pot.
5. Peel the garlic; add it to the pot and mash with the potatoes, rosemary, and sour cream. Season with salt and pepper and keep warm over low heat.
6. To make the mushroom gravy, heat the olive oil over medium-high heat. Add the onion and mushrooms and cook until they begin to brown, about 10 minutes. Add the wine and herbs de Provence; bring to a simmer. Cook until the liquid is reduced by half, about 15 minutes. Stir in the sour cream, season with salt and pepper, and keep warm over low heat.
7. To complete the dish, combine the bread crumbs, Panko, salt, pepper, and thyme leaves in a pie plate. Dredge the tofu in the bread crumb mixture, pressing the crumbs to adhere. Heat the vegetable oil in a nonstick frying pan over medium-high heat. Add the breaded tofu and fry until golden brown, about 3 minutes per side.
8. Place a mound of the mashed potatoes in the middle of 4 plates, place two or three triangles of tofu leaning on the potatoes, spoon the gravy over the top, and serve.

* Panko is a Japanese-style rice-based breading mixture found in the Asian section of most grocery stores.

Butternut Squash– and Bacon-Stuffed Crepes

4 main course servings, 6 to 8 appetizer servings

At Simpatica Dining Hall, Chef Jason Owens serves these hearty squash-filled crepes as appetizers, but they could also be served as an entrée with a salad. This is an ideal recipe for using any type of leftover roasted winter squash.

One 2-pound butternut squash, or 4 cups leftover roasted squash
2 tablespoons olive oil, divided
2 slices thick-cut bacon, cut into ½-inch pieces
1 cup chopped onion
2 tablespoons minced garlic
1 cup half-and-half
1 cup all-purpose flour
4 eggs
1 teaspoon salt
2 teaspoons butter, melted, divided
1 teaspoon minced chives
2 tablespoons Italian parsley, minced
Salt and freshly ground black pepper
2 ounces crème fraîche or sour cream, for garnish

1. Preheat the oven to 350°F and line a baking sheet with parchment paper. Halve the butternut squash lengthwise: insert a chef's knife through the center of the bulb-shaped end and cut through it, rotating the squash and cutting through the slender neck end to split it. Scrape out the seeds and stringy bits. Brush the halves with 1 tablespoon of the oil and place them cut side down on the prepared baking sheet. Bake until the squash pierces easily with a paring knife, about 1 hour. When cool enough to handle, peel the skin and discard.
2. Heat the remaining oil in a large ovenproof sauté pan or cast iron skillet over medium heat until hot. Add the bacon and onion; cook until the onion is soft and the bacon is golden brown, about 10 minutes. Add the garlic and cook for 1 minute.

3. Add the squash to the pan, combine the ingredients, and transfer to the oven. Bake, stirring occasionally, until the squash is caramelized, about 45 minutes.
4. Meanwhile, make the crepes. Combine the half-and-half, flour, eggs, and 1 teaspoon of the butter in a food processor, or whisk in a large bowl. Allow the batter to rest for 20 minutes. Strain through a fine-mesh sieve and whisk in the chives.
5. Lightly coat a 12-inch nonstick skillet with the remaining butter and heat over medium until hot. Pour a scant ¼ cup of batter into the center of the pan and swirl so the batter covers the bottom. Cook until the crepe is golden brown, about 40 seconds per side. Put on a plate and cover with foil to keep warm. Use all the batter.
6. Remove the squash mixture from the oven and stir in the parsley, salt, and pepper. Spread about ½ cup of the filling on each crepe, fold in half, top with a dollop of crème fraîche, and serve warm.

Rattlesnake Beans and Sausages

4 servings

Shelling beans require more labor than dried beans, but don't let the shelling stop you. They yield tender, flavorful beans that need less cooking time than their dried brethren. The rattlesnake beans I use have cream-white pods with mottled red and green stripes; other shelling beans such as red striped cranberry, dragon's tongue, or light green cannellini work in this recipe too. Buy pods that are leathery on the outside with plump beans on the inside, and store them in an open plastic bag in the refrigerator for up to 2 days.

2 tablespoons olive oil, divided
4 Italian or other mild sausages
2 ounces pancetta or bacon, cut into ¼-inch dice
1 cup finely chopped onion
1 medium carrot, peeled and chopped
2 teaspoons minced garlic
¼ cup dry white wine
2 pounds (about 2 cups) rattlesnake beans, shelled
⅔ cup tomato sauce
2 cups chicken stock
1 tablespoon minced fresh sage leaves, or 1½ teaspoons dry sage
1 teaspoon salt
Freshly ground black pepper

1. Heat 1 tablespoon of the oil over medium-high heat in a heavy-bottomed saucepan. Add the sausages and cook until they are well browned. Remove them from the pan and set aside.
2. In the same pan, add the remaining oil and fry the pancetta until it is crisp. Add the onion and carrot, and cook until the onion is translucent, about 8 minutes. Add the garlic and cook for 1 minute. Deglaze the pan with the wine and simmer for 2 minutes, scraping up the browned bits from the bottom.
3. Stir in the beans, tomato sauce, stock, sage, and salt; nestle the sausages among the beans and bring to a simmer over medium-high heat. Reduce the heat and simmer gently for 10 minutes. (Do not boil the beans or they will quickly turn to mush.)
4. Bite into a bean. If the center is firm and chalky, continue to cook until the beans are tender but still have a bit of chew, 10 to 20 minutes depending on the bean. Season with salt and pepper and serve.

Fettuccine with Porcini Cream Sauce

4 servings

Porcini mushrooms, though costly, have a delicate, earthy flavor that is best paired with uncomplicated ingredients to allow their character to shine. Fresh pasta and a simple cream sauce offer a great stage for fall's best, plumpest porcinis.

2 tablespoons butter
⅓ cup finely chopped shallots
½ teaspoon minced garlic
1 pinch red chili flakes
4 to 6 ounces fresh porcini mushrooms*, sliced
3 cups cream
¾ pound fresh fettuccine or papparadelle
Salt and freshly ground black pepper
2 ounces (½ cup) Parmesan cheese, grated

1. Heat the butter in a large saucepan over medium heat. Add the shallots and sauté until they begin to brown, about 8 minutes. Add the garlic and chili flakes, and cook for 1 minute.
2. Add the mushrooms and cook until they begin to break down and become tender, about 10 minutes. Add the cream, reduce the heat to medium-low, and simmer for 15 minutes.
3. Meanwhile, bring a large pot of salted water to a boil. Add the pasta and cook until al dente; reserve 1 cup of the liquid and drain.
4. Add the pasta to the cream sauce and toss with tongs. Remove from the heat, season with salt and pepper, and allow the mixture to stand for 1 minute. The sauce will thicken as it cools; add the reserved pasta liquid if needed. Serve the pasta in bowls and the cheese on the side.

* If fresh porcini mushrooms are not available, use good-quality dried porcinis (see Resources). Cover 2 ounces of dried porcinis with boiling water and steep for 30 minutes. Remove from the water, roughly chop, and proceed with the recipe. For extra flavor, pour the soaking liquid through a fine sieve lined with a paper towel and add up to ½ cup to the sauce.

How to Choose: Porcini mushrooms, sometimes called cèpes, appear at markets in the fall and occasionally the spring. The spongy layer under the chestnut-colored caps should be relatively dry; avoid any that are sticky or smelly. Inspect porcinis carefully before purchase and avoid those with many tiny holes—bugs have been there. Cut away any areas under the cap that are mushy or green. Refrigerate on a paper towel–lined plate and use within 2 days of purchase.

Wild Salmon with Corn, Cherry Tomato, and Artichoke Sauté

4 servings

Artichokes come to market around March and sometimes stay until May. Their flavor matches up perfectly with other bud-like spring edibles like asparagus, peas, and fava beans. In the Pacific Northwest they come to market again in October, and they blend just as well with fall's earthy flavors like corn, cherry tomatoes, and salmon.

The debate over wild versus farmed salmon rages, especially in the Pacific Northwest. Though there are a few salmon farms that raise fish sustainably, I prefer to buy wild local salmon for its superior flavor and less damaging environmental impact. For more information about the plight of the world's salmon stocks, consult the Ecotrust's Salmon Nation Web site listed on page 223.

1 large globe artichoke
Juice of 1 lemon, divided
2 slices thick-cut bacon, diced
1 tablespoon olive oil
3 ears sweet corn, shucked and cut off cobs (about 2½ cups)
1 cup cherry tomatoes
½ cup basil leaves, torn into small pieces
Salt and freshly ground black pepper
2 teaspoons vegetable oil
Four 4- to 6-ounce wild salmon fillets, skin on

1. Cut the leaves off the artichoke just above the base. With a sharp paring knife, peel away the stringy green stem layer and any remaining tough green leaves still attached to the base. Quarter the artichoke lengthwise and cut away the fluffy choke in the center, rubbing cut areas with half of the lemon juice to prevent browning. Thinly slice the artichoke and place the slices in a bowl of cold water with the remaining lemon juice; set aside.
2. In a large sauté pan, cook the bacon over medium-high heat until it browns and renders most of its fat; add the olive oil if necessary to make 2 tablespoons of fat. Reduce the heat to medium, drain the artichoke slices well, and add them to the pan. Sauté until the slices begin to brown on the edges and are tender, 5 to 8 minutes.

3. Add the corn and tomatoes and sauté briefly until the corn turns bright yellow and is crisp-tender. Stir in the basil and salt and pepper to taste. Pour the mixture into a bowl and cover loosely with foil.
4. Wipe the sauté pan with a paper towel, heat over high heat, and pour in the vegetable oil. Season the salmon generously with salt and pepper and place in the pan, skin side up. Sear them for 3 minutes, reduce the heat to medium, and carefully turn them over. Continue to cook until they are medium rare, about 3 minutes depending on thickness (see *, page 82).
5. Carefully place the fillets on dinner plates, top with the corn sauté, and serve.

How to Choose: Artichokes are best eaten as close to the time of harvest as possible. A fresh artichoke will give a little squeak when squeezed. Choose large, compact artichokes with fresh-looking stems. The bracts (leaves) should be deep green, closed tightly, and not shriveled. If the leaves are beginning to open, the artichoke is past its prime. Wrap artichokes loosely in a plastic bag and store in the vegetable keeper for up to 4 days.

Seared Black Cod in Tomato Broth

4 servings

Chef Ben Stenn of Celilo Restaurant and Bar in picturesque Hood River, Oregon, developed this recipe to use a bumper crop of overripe tomatoes a farmer brought him. "Bruised, discolored, or otherwise unattractive tomatoes work best for the broth . . . market vendors love when you buy their last basket of beat-up fall tomatoes no one else wants," he says.

Black cod, also called butterfish or sablefish, is a white fish from the Pacific Northwest coast with a buttery yet firm texture. The Monterey Bay Aquarium's Seafood Watch organization (see information, page 223) rates Alaska- and Canadian-caught black cod in its "best choice" category for those aiming toward sustainable fish consumption.

Cheesecloth or a flour sack dish towel, for straining
5 pounds ripe tomatoes
1 teaspoon kosher salt
1 long piece kitchen string
1 pint cherry or pear tomatoes, halved
Salt
White pepper
2 tablespoons vegetable oil
2 pounds black cod or other firm white fish
Freshly ground black pepper
4 sprigs chervil or basil

1. Line a large mixing bowl with 4 layers of the cheesecloth, leaving enough excess to drape over the sides. Quarter the ripe tomatoes and pulse them in a blender in two or three batches; pour the puree into the cheesecloth-lined bowl. Stir in the kosher salt.
2. Carefully gather the edges of the cheesecloth to form a bundle. Tie it closed with the string.
3. Suspend the bundle in the refrigerator over a glass mixing bowl or stainless steel stock pot. Allow it to hang for 24 hours without being disturbed; the weight of the tomatoes and gravity will cause a clear tomato broth to drip through the cloth and collect in the bowl.
4. Put the tomato broth and cherry tomatoes in a medium saucepan over low heat and gently warm, but do not boil. Season with salt and white pepper. (Reserve the drained tomato purée for another use such as pasta sauce.)

▸ *continued*

5. Heat the oil in a large sauté pan or skillet until it is hot but not smoking. Season the fish with salt and black pepper and place it in the pan skin side up. Reduce the heat to medium-high; cook until the bottom is golden brown, about 4 minutes. Carefully turn the cod over and sear until it is cooked through, 3 to 5 minutes depending on thickness (see *, page 82).
6. Carefully remove the fish from the pan and pat it dry with paper towels to remove excess oil. Place the fillets in 4 warm bowls and gently spoon the broth mixture around the fish. Garnish each bowl with the chervil and serve.

Roasted Duck Breast with Bourbon-Braised Italian Prunes

4 servings

Chef Jason Wilson of Crush dries fresh Italian plums (also called fresh Italian prunes) to garnish this sweet-savory dish. Find Italian prunes already dried at some orchard stands and farmer's market stalls where plums are sold; standard dried prunes work as well. Chef Wilson serves this dish with roasted brussels sprouts with bacon and cream.

FOR THE DUCK BREASTS:

½ teaspoon fennel seeds
¼ teaspoon dried lavender blossoms
¼ teaspoon ground coriander
½ teaspoon freshly ground black pepper
2 teaspoons kosher salt
Zest of 1 orange
2 teaspoons fresh thyme leaves
3 duck breasts
½ cup good-quality bourbon, such as Maker's Mark, divided

FOR THE PRUNES:

2 tablespoons butter
2 tablespoons minced shallots
½ cup chicken stock
6 sprigs fresh thyme
Zest of 2 oranges
⅛ teaspoon Espelette pepper*
1 cinnamon stick
1 cup (5 ounces) dried Italian prunes
Salt
Freshly ground black pepper

1. Grind the fennel seeds and lavender in a clean spice grinder or mortar and pestle and combine with the coriander, black pepper, salt, orange zest, and thyme leaves. With a sharp knife score the duck skin to make a crisscross pattern. Rub each duck breast with 1 tablespoon of the bourbon and some of the spice mixture; marinate on a large dinner plate at room temperature while making the prunes.

continued

2. Preheat the oven to 400°F. Bring the butter, shallots, stock, thyme, orange zest, Espelette pepper, and cinnamon stick to a boil in a small saucepan. Add the prunes and the remaining bourbon; cover and simmer over medium-low heat until the prunes are plump, about 30 minutes. Season with salt and keep warm.
3. Heat a large ovenproof sauté pan or cast iron skillet over medium heat until warm. Place the duck breasts skin side down in the pan and cook until the fat under the skin has rendered into the pan and the skin is crisp and deep golden brown, 15 to 20 minutes.
4. Turn the duck breasts over, put the pan in the oven, and continue to cook until an instant-read thermometer registers 135°F when inserted into the thickest part of the meat, 4 to 8 minutes depending on size of duck breast.**
5. Transfer the duck to a large plate and allow to rest for 5 minutes. Uncover the prunes, bring to a simmer, and allow the liquid to reduce by half, to about ½ cup. Season with salt and black pepper to taste.
6. With a sharp knife, slice the duck at a 45-degree angle. Fan the slices on 4 plates, place 4 prunes on each plate, drizzle with the prune cooking liquid, and serve.

* Espelette pepper is made from a pimento-like pepper grown in the Basque region of southwestern France. The hot, smoky flavor is worth seeking out, but hot paprika can be used as a substitute. See Resources for details.

** The duck in this recipe is cooked to medium. For accuracy, I recommend using an instant-read thermometer when cooking meats. They are available at kitchen supply stores.

Roasted Pork and Apples with Cream Gravy

4 to 6 servings

The pork sold in supermarkets today is so lean that it bears no resemblance to the juicy, flavorful pork roasts my grandmother served for Sunday dinners. Fortunately, chefs and consumers are creating a demand for healthy free-range pork that has sufficient marbling to make tasty roasts and chops. The best place to find good pork is at your local farmer's market where conscientious livestock farmers can get a fair price for their meat away from the cutthroat commodities market.

One 3 to 4 pound pork loin roast
Kosher salt and freshly ground black pepper
1 tablespoon olive oil
8 small (4 ounces) shallots, peeled and whole
Two 4-inch sprigs fresh rosemary
1 bay leaf
2 sweet-tart baking apples such as Braeburn or Granny Smith, halved and cored
½ cup hard apple cider*
1 pint cream

1. Preheat the oven to 400°F. Season the roast on all sides with salt and pepper. Heat the oil in a Dutch oven or ovenproof pan over high heat. Sear the pork on all sides until it is deep brown, carefully turning with tongs. Transfer to a plate. Arrange the shallots, rosemary, and bay leaf in the Dutch oven and place the pork on top. Cover with foil and bake for 40 minutes.
2. Remove the foil, nestle the apples around the pork, and continue to roast until an instant-read thermometer inserted in the center of the roast reads 145°F, 20 to 40 minutes depending on the size of the roast (the pork should have a blush of pink juice when sliced). Remove from the oven, place the pork on a cutting board, and cover it loosely with the foil.
3. Put the shallots and apples in a small serving bowl and keep warm. Over high heat deglaze the Dutch oven with the cider, scraping any browned bits on the bottom and sides of the pan; reduce the liquid by half. Add the cream and simmer until thickened, about 2 minutes. Season with salt and pepper.
4. Carve the roast and serve with the shallots, apples, and cream gravy.

* Hard cider is fermented apple cider; it can be found in bottles wherever beer is sold. You can substitute apple cider, if you prefer.

Shredded Brussels Sprouts with Red Pepper Vinaigrette

6 side dish servings

Thinly slicing brussels sprouts produces a dish with a buttery flavor akin to sautéed cabbage. Be careful not to overcook the slices; brussels sprouts get a skunky-cabbage taste when they are cooked too long. If you think you don't like brussels sprouts, this quick stir-fry will change your mind.

1 pound brussels sprouts
1 cup roasted red bell peppers (see recipe, page 75)
1 tablespoon apple cider or sherry vinegar
1 pinch salt
2 tablespoons extra virgin olive oil
1 tablespoon vegetable oil
3 tablespoons thinly sliced shallots
Freshly ground black pepper

1. Swish the brussels sprouts with cold water in a large bowl and drain in a large colander. Halve each sprout lengthwise through the root end from top to bottom, then shred into ⅛-inch-thick pieces.
2. To make the vinaigrette, blend the bell peppers, vinegar, and salt in a blender. With the blender running, slowly pour in the olive oil in a steady stream; set aside.
3. Heat a wok or large sauté pan over high heat. Add the vegetable oil and shallots and cook until they just begin to brown, about 3 minutes. Add the sprouts, sprinkle with salt and pepper, and toss constantly with a spatula and wide wooden spoon until the shreds are just tender, 3 to 5 minutes.
4. Remove the wok from the heat and add enough vinaigrette to lightly coat the sprouts. Serve hot as a side dish. Refrigerate leftover vinaigrette in an airtight container for up to 1 week; shake well before using on salads, roasted meats, or vegetables.

How to Choose: The freshest, mildest brussels sprouts come still attached to their thick stalks. Whether or not you buy them attached, they should have bright green, compact heads and be no larger than unshelled walnuts. Brussels sprouts with yellow or split leaves are old and should be avoided. Use them within a few days of purchase for the best flavor; they become more sulfurous with age.

Fingerling Potato and Jerusalem Artichoke Gratin

6 side dish servings

Jerusalem artichokes, also known as sunchokes, don't have anything to do with Jerusalem, but they do have a buttery flavor something like an artichoke heart. When raw, their crisp, water chestnut–like texture adds a nice crunch to salads and relishes. When baked they become buttery and tender, as with this simple gratin. Fingerling potatoes are small with an irregular, finger-like shape. There are many varieties—French fingerling, Austrian Crescent, Russian banana; all have a rich texture and flavor and are good roasted, steamed, or baked.

1¼ cups milk or cream
1 bay leaf
1 large garlic clove, peeled
1 tablespoon olive oil
⅔ cup sliced shallots
2 tablespoons butter, at room temperature
1½ pounds fingerling or Yukon gold potatoes, scrubbed
½ pound Jerusalem artichokes, peeled
2 cups shredded cow's milk cheese, such as fontina or Gruyère, divided
Salt and freshly ground black pepper
Freshly grated nutmeg

1. Preheat the oven to 425°F. Warm the milk, bay leaf, and garlic in a small saucepan over medium heat until hot. Reduce heat to low and keep warm.
2. Heat the oil in a large ovenproof skillet or sauté pan over medium-high heat. Add the shallots and cook until they are golden brown, about 3 minutes. Transfer them to a small bowl and set aside.

3. With a mandoline or chef's knife, slice the potatoes ⅛ inch thick and place them in a medium bowl of cold water to prevent them from oxidizing. Thinly slice the artichokes and add them to the potatoes.
4. Drain well and layer half the potato mixture in the skillet. Sprinkle with half the cheese, shallots, salt, and pepper. Top with the remaining potato mixture. Pour the milk over all, then sprinkle with the remaining cheese, salt, pepper, and nutmeg.
5. Cook over medium-high heat until the milk begins to bubble around the edges, about 6 minutes. Transfer the skillet to the oven and bake until the potatoes are tender and the top is brown and crusty, about 30 minutes. Serve hot from the skillet as a side dish for roasted chicken or grilled meat.

How to Choose: Jerusalem artichokes (sunchokes) are at the market from midfall to early spring. They have dark brown or beige skin and multiple fingers extending from a roundish center, making them difficult to wash and peel. Pick those with relatively few protrusions and a firm texture with no squishy spots. Keep them in a brown paper bag in the vegetable keeper for up to 2 weeks.

Roasted Roots with Gremolata Butter

4 servings

I frequently roast a mix of root vegetables for a quick weeknight side dish. The same carrot-potato-onion combination can get old though; for variety, I use different roots and toss them with a butter flavored with garlic, parsley, and lemon zest for a nice departure from the usual root-roast. The quantity looks huge when you're preparing it, but the vegetables will shrink considerably as they roast.

1 pound mixed root vegetables (yams, parsnips, salsify, carrots, Jerusalem artichokes, rutabaga), peeled
1 pound fingerling potatoes, scrubbed
3 tablespoons extra virgin olive oil
1 tablespoon chopped fresh rosemary
Salt and freshly ground black pepper
2 tablespoons Italian parsley leaves
1 large garlic clove
Zest of 1 lemon
2 tablespoons butter, at room temperature

1. Place a heavy rimmed baking sheet in the oven and preheat the oven to 400°F. Cut the root vegetables and potatoes into equal-size sticks ¼ inch thick and 3 inches long. In a large bowl, toss them with the oil, rosemary, and generous sprinkles of salt and pepper.
2. Pull out the oven rack that holds the preheated baking sheet and tip the mixture onto the hot pan, which sears the mixture and reduces the likelihood of sticking. Roast the vegetables, stirring once halfway through cooking, until the pieces are tender, 25 to 30 minutes.
3. Meanwhile, place the parsley, garlic, and lemon zest on a cutting board with a generous pinch of salt, and finely mince. Stir the mixture with the butter. Toss the vegetables with the butter mixture and serve.

How to Choose: Rumored to be Thomas Jefferson's favorite root vegetable, salsify looks quite humble—to most it's just a dirty white carrot with loads of filament-type roots. The flavor, however, is buttery when roasted, sweet and mellow when peeled into thin strips and deep fried for a garnish, and silky-subtle when mashed with potatoes. Choose salsify that is firm and of moderate size; the thicker it is, the tougher the texture. Refrigerate salsify wrapped loosely in a plastic bag for up to 4 weeks; use while still firm and crisp.

Farro with Lobster Mushrooms

8 side dish servings

Chef Johnathan Sundstrom offers a wide range of market-driven dishes in a small-plate format at his restaurant, Lark. This hearty dish of farro—a nutty Italian grain related to spelt—and meaty lobster mushrooms is a fall favorite. Chef Sundstrom gets his farro from Bluebird Grain Farms in Winthrop, Washington, one of the few sources for domestically grown farro. The farm's products are available at some Seattle-area farmer's markets and by mail (see Resources). Whole spelt, available at health food stores, can be substituted.

4 tablespoons olive oil, divided
½ cup finely chopped onion
2 cups farro or spelt
3 cups hot water or stock
½ cup (4 ounces) mascarpone cheese
Salt and freshly ground black pepper
¾ pound lobster mushrooms, cleaned and sliced ½ inch thick
1 tablespoon butter
½ cup dry white wine
2 tablespoons minced chives

1. Heat 2 tablespoons of the oil in a large saucepan over medium-high heat. Add the onion and cook until it becomes translucent, about 8 minutes. Stir in the farro and cook for 1 minute to toast it, stirring constantly.
2. Add the water and bring to a simmer. Reduce the heat to medium-low, cover, and cook until the farro is tender, 30 to 40 minutes. Stir in the mascarpone, season with salt and pepper, and keep warm over very low heat.

3. In a large sauté pan, heat the remaining oil over high heat until it begins to shimmer. Add the mushrooms and cook without stirring until they become crisp around the edges. Turn them with tongs and continue to cook until crisp, about 2 minutes. Turn off the heat; add the butter, toss to coat the mushrooms, season with salt and pepper, and set aside in a small bowl.
4. Put the sauté pan over high heat; add the wine, scrape up any browned mushroom bits stuck to the bottom of the pan, and simmer until the wine is reduced by half. Stir into the farro mixture.
5. Put the farro into a serving dish. Top with the mushrooms and chives and serve.

How to Choose: Lobster mushrooms are easy to spot midsummer to late fall—their knobby shape and flame-orange color, a bit like a lobster's shell, distinguish them from other mushrooms. Their dense, firm texture is good for sautéing, marinating, and grilling. Some say the flavor is something like seafood, though I find it to be more smoky sweet. Pick fairly dry mushrooms with no mushy spots. Though the color is generally flame orange, a few black specks are common as well. Avoid mushrooms with tiny holes as they indicate the presence of insects; when the mushrooms are infested, they tend to be very infested. To clean, spray them with water and scrub with a baby's toothbrush. Refrigerate in a paper bag for up to 5 days.

Garnet Yams with Hazelnut Butter

4 to 6 side dish servings

This recipe for yams is light years away from the cloyingly sweet, marshmallow-topped yam dishes from Thanksgiving meals of yore. The earthy-sweet flavor of yams shines through, augmented with a rich hazelnut butter and the crunch of green onion. Try this as a side dish for lamb chops or pork.

3 pounds Garnet, Jewel, Beauregard, or other moist, orange-fleshed yams
4 tablespoons vegetable oil, divided
1 teaspoon salt
Freshly ground black pepper
1 cup hazelnuts
½ cup (1 stick) butter, at room temperature
2 green onions, chopped

1. Preheat the oven to 400°F. Peel the yams and cut them into 3-inch-long wedges. Place them on a rimmed baking sheet; toss with 2 tablespoons of the oil, salt, and pepper. Bake until they are tender when pierced with a fork, about 40 minutes.
2. Toast the hazelnuts in the oven on a rimmed baking sheet for 10 to 15 minutes, until the nuts are colored lightly and the skins crack. When cool enough to handle, rub small handfuls between your palms over the sink to loosen their papery skins.
3. Transfer the hazelnuts to a blender or small food processor. Add the butter and the remaining oil and blend until smooth, stopping to scrape down the sides.
4. Transfer the yams to a serving bowl, toss with about half the hazelnut butter and green onions, and serve. Refrigerate the remaining hazelnut butter in an airtight container for several weeks; use on toast, vegetables, and sautés.

How to Choose: Distinguishing a sweet potato from a yam is a tricky business. Garnet, Jewel, and Beauregard yams are sweet potatoes bred to deliver the moist, sweet orange flesh Americans prefer to the pale, dry flesh of sweet potatoes. Years ago some enterprising sweet potato farmers decided to set apart their Garnet-style sweet potatoes by renaming them yams, so some sweet potatoes are now called yams even though they are not at all related to the dry, starchy yams of South America.

Beet and Cardoon Gratin

4 to 6 side dish servings

Executive Chef Kenny Giambalvo gets raves for this unusual gratin of cardoons and beets at his Portland restaurant, Bluehour. If you use red beets, their color will bleed into the cream and make the dish a stunning crimson color. Yellow beets will lend a less colorful effect.

Cardoons, a relative of globe artichokes, are a favorite in Mediterranean countries for their pale green celery-like stalks and savory flavor similar to artichokes. In Italy, cardoon stalks are served raw with a butter-anchovy-garlic dip, deep fried, or baked in gratins. Though they take a little time to prepare (the leaves are inedible; the stalks need to be peeled, and most cardoons grown in the United States must be blanched before eating), their flavor is an epiphany for artichoke fans. When you find cardoons at the farmer's market, support their cultivation by buying a bunch of the Dr. Seuss–esque stalks.

1 tablespoon butter, at room temperature
2 pounds cardoon stalks with leaves
Cold water, for blanching
Juice from 1 lemon
1 pound red or yellow beets, peeled and sliced ⅛ inch thick
Salt and freshly ground black pepper
Freshly grated nutmeg
Zest of 1 orange
⅔ cup finely chopped shallots
2 teaspoons finely chopped garlic
1 cup grated Parmesan cheese, divided
3 cups heavy cream, divided

1. Preheat the oven to 350°F and butter the bottom and sides of a 2-quart baking dish. Wash the cardoons well and cut away all the leaves and thorny bits. In a large bowl, combine the water and lemon juice. With a sharp vegetable peeler, peel away the stringy fibers that run the length of the cardoon stalks and slice the stalks on a bias into ½-inch-thick pieces, placing the slices in the lemon water to prevent them from oxidizing.
2. Bring a pot of salted to water to a boil. Add the cardoon pieces and cook until just tender, 10 to 15 minutes depending on age and size of the stalks. Drain and set aside.

▸ *continued*

3. Arrange a layer of beet slices in the prepared baking dish. Season with a little salt, pepper, nutmeg, orange zest, shallots, garlic, and Parmesan. Top with a layer of cardoons and drizzle with ½ cup of the cream. Continue to layer until all the beets and cardoons are used, finishing with the cardoons, remaining cream, and a generous sprinkle of Parmesan, but leaving at least ½ inch of space at the top.
4. Place the baking dish on a baking sheet, cover with foil, and bake until the beets are fork tender, about 40 minutes. Remove the foil and continue baking until golden brown on top, about 20 minutes. Allow the gratin to rest for 15 minutes before serving.

How to Choose: Cardoons come into season in late fall, with an occasional crop in early spring. Buy the small, firm, innermost stalks if possible. For every 3 to 4 pounds of leafy cardoon stalks, you'll end up with about 1½ pounds of edible vegetable. Before using, cardoons must be blanched to remove some of their bitterness. If you can't find them at your local farmer's market, you might have better luck asking someone in your neighborhood—they are a popular ornamental plant.

Schiacciata (Sweet Grape Focaccia)

8 servings

Sweet focaccia dimpled with plump grapes is sold by the slice everywhere in Italy during the grape harvest, when grapes are at their juiciest. The name *schiacciata* means "squashed" in Italian, referring to how the grapes are pushed into the dough. Artisan bread baker Tim Healea has reinvented this Old World recipe; he uses grapes from the Willamette Valley wine country to create this treat for Pearl Bakery.

1⅓ cups warm water
1½ teaspoons active dry yeast
¼ cup plus 2 tablespoons olive oil, divided
3¾ cups unbleached all-purpose flour, divided
32 large seedless black or red grapes
1 teaspoon anise seeds
1 tablespoon sugar
1 tablespoon turbinado sugar*

1. Mix the water and yeast in the bowl of a heavy-duty electric mixer and allow to stand until the mixture is creamy and the yeast has dissolved, about 10 minutes.
2. Add ¼ cup of the oil and 1 cup of the flour; blend with the paddle attachment. Gradually add the remaining flour 1 cup at a time. Switch to the dough hook and knead on low speed for 3 minutes; turn the dough onto a floured board and knead by hand for 3 minutes. (Alternatively, make the dough by hand: mix the ingredients with a spoon and knead for 10 minutes on a lightly floured surface.)
3. Brush a baking sheet with a little oil and put the dough on it. Cover with a clean dish towel and allow to rest in a warm place until the dough has doubled in volume, about 1 hour.
4. Preheat the oven to 450°F. Transfer the dough to a floured surface and cut it in half. Push down the dough with the heel of your hand and stretch the halves into ovals about 12 inches long and ½ inch thick. Return both halves to the baking sheet, brush with the remaining oil, and push the grapes into each half, spacing them ¾ inch apart. Sprinkle each half with the anise seeds and sugars. Allow to rise for 20 minutes.
5. Bake until the bottom is golden brown, about 30 minutes. Cut it into squares and serve warm.

* Turbinado sugar is coarse, raw sugar that has a light molasses flavor. It retains its texture during baking, giving a slight crunch and attractive sparkle to the bread. You'll find it in most supermarkets labeled as turbinado or raw sugar. If it's not available, substitute regular sugar.

A Pear Primer

More than 5,000 varieties of pears are grown around the world, so it's a matter of trial and error to find your favorites. If there are orchards in your area, I recommend you try some of the heirloom pears and apples that are gaining attention for their distinct flavors and textures. You'll never go back to rock hard, flavorless mega-supermarket pears or apples.

Pears are picked before they become ripe. To ripen them at home, place them in a bowl and keep them at room temperature. Test for ripeness by pushing gently near the stem; it will give slightly when ripe. Once ripe, store pears in an open paper bag, refrigerate, and use within a few days. Pears absorb odors, so don't bunk them with cut onions or the like.

1. and 2. **RED AND YELLOW BARTLETT:** Bartletts are one of few pears that change color when ripe—from dull burgundy to bright red or light green to bright yellow, respectively. The fruity aroma of these popular pears will get your attention at farmer's markets from late August into November. They are sweet and juicy, good for eating raw on their own or in salads.

3. **BOSC:** An elegant-looking pear with a long, tapered neck and rich golden to golden brown skin, these pears have a dense flesh and thick skin that make them ideal for baking and poaching.

4. **TAYLOR'S GOLD:** These large, golden brown pears have a light green undertone with a thick skin similar to Boscs. The flesh is extremely juicy, sweet, and complex. They make great sorbet when stewed with cinnamon and sugar syrup.

5. **COMICE:** These large, round pears have a thin green skin with a red blush on one side. They are extremely juicy with a sweet flesh that has a pronounced pear flavor. Try them with a young sheep's milk cheese for dessert.

6. **ASIAN:** This name is given to many firm, round pears with a rich golden color and crisp flesh. The most common is the Twentieth Century variety, or Nijisseiki, a juicy pear with a slightly tart finish. Asian pears can keep in the refrigerator for months but will acquire a tannic flavor when kept too long.

7. and 8. **RED AND GREEN ANJOU:** A round French variety with a short neck, these hardy pears appear in late fall and are usually available until spring. They have a fine-textured, mild flesh with just a hint of astringency, especially near the skin. They're good for salads or roasted with pork.

9. **STARKRIMSON:** A sexy crimson pear that becomes even brighter when ripe, its juicy, smooth flesh and slightly floral aroma pairs well with salty cheeses. Try a Starkrimson halved, cored, and filled with chopped walnuts and local blue cheese.

10. **FORELLE:** These small, bright yellow pears sport crimson freckles when ripe. Sweet and very juicy, they are great on peanut butter sandwiches or in salads.

Toffee Apple Upside Down Cake

8 servings

This recipe, contributed by Pastry Chef Melissa Lehmkuhl of ROUX, is the perfect start to apple season. As the cake bakes, the rich spice mixture will fill your home with the intoxicating aromas of cinnamon, nutmeg, and allspice. Leftovers can be served as a coffee cake at breakfast time.

FOR THE CARAMEL TOFFEE LAYER:

- ¾ cup cup plus 2 tablespoons granulated sugar
- 1 pinch salt
- 3 tablespoons unsalted butter

FOR THE CAKE:

- 3 cups all purpose flour
- 1½ teaspoons baking powder
- ¾ teaspoon baking soda
- 1 teaspoon salt
- 2½ teaspoons ground cinnamon
- ¾ teaspoon freshly grated nutmeg
- ½ teaspoon ground allspice
- ½ teaspoon ground cardamom
- ½ teaspoon ground mace
- 1½ cups granulated sugar
- ⅓ cup firmly packed brown sugar
- 3 eggs
- 1 cup vegetable oil
- 6 tablespoons unsalted butter, melted
- 1 tablespoon vanilla extract
- 4 large (2 pounds) Granny Smith apples

1. Preheat the oven to 350° F. Spray a 9- or 10-inch springform pan with nonstick cooking spray.
2. Melt the sugar and salt in a small saucepan over medium-high heat, stirring constantly with a wooden spoon. The sugar will clump as it begins to melt; keep stirring until the sugar is liquid and turns a light amber color. This change will happen suddenly (roughly 30 seconds), so be vigilant and remove the pan from the heat immediately when the sugar colors. Stir the butter into the pan a few bits at a time until incorporated. Carefully pour the mixture into the springform pan.

3. Whisk the flour, baking powder, baking soda, salt, cinnamon, nutmeg, allspice, cardamom, and mace in a large bowl.
4. In a separate bowl, beat the sugars and eggs for 3 minutes. Add the oil, butter, and vanilla and combine.
5. Add the flour mixture to the wet mixture in 2 batches and stir until just incorporated.
6. Peel, core, and grate 3 apples (about 3 cups) and fold into the batter with a rubber spatula. Peel and core the remaining apple and slice into ½-inch-thick wedges; arrange decoratively over the toffee mixture in the pan. Pour the cake batter over the apples.
7. Put the pan on a baking sheet and bake until a wooden skewer inserted in the center comes out clean, about 1 hour and 30 minutes. Allow the cake to cool for 30 minutes, carefully invert onto a serving plate, remove pan bottom, and serve warm.

Poached Pear and Hazelnut Tart

6 to 8 servings

Pearl Bakery sells European-style pastries and breads made with local ingredients, both at their shop and at the Portland Farmer's Market. Pastry Chef Lee Posey created this fabulous pear tart as an autumn special for the bakery. For poaching, Chef Posey chooses pears that are just shy of ripe. "When there are tiny wrinkles around the stem area, they're ready to go."

FOR THE TART CRUST:

1½ cups all-purpose flour
¼ cup sugar
¼ teaspoon kosher salt
½ cup (1 stick) cold unsalted butter, cut into ½-inch chunks
2 egg yolks

FOR THE POACHED PEARS:

1 cup dry Marsala wine
½ cup water
¾ cup sugar
1 cinnamon stick
Juice and zest of 1 orange
1 vanilla bean, or 1 teaspoon vanilla extract
3 large (about 1¼ pounds) Bosc pears

FOR THE HAZELNUT FILLING:

¾ cup hazelnuts, toasted and skinned (see instructions, page 146)
5 tablespoons sugar
¼ cup (½ stick) unsalted butter, at room temperature
1 egg
1 egg yolk
1 teaspoon vanilla extract
3 tablespoons all-purpose flour

FOR ASSEMBLY:

2 teaspoons sugar
1 teaspoons ground cinnamon
¼ cup apricot preserves

1. To make the tart shell, blend the flour, sugar, salt, and butter in the bowl of an electric mixer with the paddle attachment or in a food processor until the butter is in small chunks no larger than peas. Whisk the egg yolks in a small measuring cup; add enough water to make ¼ cup liquid and add to the flour mixture. Mix until the dough just starts to come together. Gather the dough, shape it into a disc, and wrap in plastic wrap. Chill for at least 1 hour or up to 3 days.
2. Allow the tart dough to stand at room temperature for 5 minutes. On a lightly floured surface, roll the dough into a ⅛-inch-thick disc, frequently rotating it to prevent sticking. Transfer to an 8- or 9-inch tart pan with a removable bottom. Push the dough snugly into the pan, leaving dough hanging over the edges. Roll a rolling pin over the top to trim the edges. Freeze the shell until firm, about 30 minutes.
3. To poach the pears, in a medium saucepan combine the wine, water, sugar, cinnamon stick, orange juice, orange zest, and vanilla bean. Bring to a boil and stir to dissolve the sugar. Remove from the heat and allow the mixture to steep while preparing the pears.
4. Preheat the oven to 350°F. Peel, core, and quarter the pears, adding them to the poaching liquid as you work. Return the pan to the stove, bring to a simmer, and cook until the pears are tender when pierced with a paring knife, 10 to 15 minutes. Remove them from the liquid and allow them to cool to room temperature.
5. To make the hazelnut filling, process the nuts with the sugar in a food processor until finely ground. Add the butter and blend. Add the egg, egg yolk, and vanilla and blend. Stir in the flour by hand until combined.
6. Fill the frozen tart shell with the hazelnut filling (you may not need all of it). Arrange 8 to 10 pear quarters snugly on the filling. Blend the sugar and cinnamon and sprinkle over the pears. Bake until the tart is golden brown, about 25 minutes. Transfer tart shell to a rack and cool completely. Using a small sharp knife gently loosen the crust from sides of the pan. Push up pan bottom to release the tart.
7. Heat the preserves over low heat and brush over the tart. Cut into wedges and serve at room temperature with vanilla ice cream. The tart keeps for 2 days at room temperature.

Marsala-Baked Pears with Maple Whipped Cream

4 servings

When you want something sweet at the end of a meal, but don't want to fiddle with measuring flour and hauling out the mixer, turn to this simple roasted pear recipe. I use Marsala wine because it has a caramely aroma that matches well with the spices and orange; you can use port, dry sherry, or a not-too-sweet Riesling for this recipe as well.

¾ cup dry Marsala wine
½ cup plus 1 tablespoon sugar, divided
1 cinnamon stick, broken into pieces
5 whole cloves
1 vanilla bean
1 orange
4 semifirm Bosc pears
¾ cup cold heavy whipping cream
1 tablespoon maple syrup

1. Preheat the oven to 300°F. Combine the wine, ½ cup of the sugar, cinnamon pieces, and cloves in a small baking dish or pie plate. Split the vanilla bean lengthwise and scrape out the sticky black center with the blunt end of a paring knife; add to the wine mixture with the scraped vanilla pod.
2. Zest the orange over the baking dish to catch the zest and aromatic oils. Using a sharp paring knife, cut a slice off of the top and bottom of the orange. Cutting vertically, trim away all the rind and white pith. Slice the orange into rounds and place them in the baking dish.
3. Put the pears on top of the oranges. (Slice a bit off the bottom of the pears if they don't sit upright.) Spoon some wine mixture over each pear.
4. Bake, basting occasionally with the wine mixture, until the pears are tender when cut into with a paring knife, about 2 hours. Allow the pears to cool for 30 minutes; continue to baste them from time to time.
5. Whip the cream with the maple syrup and remaining sugar until soft peaks form. Place the pears on individual plates, spooning enough of the wine mixture over them to make them glisten. Place a dollop of whipped cream next to each pear and serve.

WINTER

AS YOU BEGIN TO SEE YOUR BREATH FLOATING IN THE MORNING AIR, market offerings become more sparse, along with the crowds. There are so few shoppers later in the season that it sometimes feels as though we've stumbled upon our own private market. Even in the worst weather, though, there's plenty to warm the belly—reassuring roots, dried mushrooms, honey, and hearty greens. Seafood becomes plentiful as the weather cools, from briny oysters to sweet Dungeness crabmeat for crab cakes. Meat vendors have cuts like pork shoulder for braising, and neighboring stalls will have huge purple cabbage to sauté with caraway seeds. In midwinter, when the damp cold really clings, reach for the soup pot and make enough creamy clam chowder or spiced Indian lentil soup to last the week. Sweet things are available too. In some places vibrant fruits still show up at the market well into December—persimmon for winter salads, tart quince, and apple cider from local orchards. Sometimes it's good to be cold, if only to be warmed again from the inside out.

meet the producer

It's the third week of January, the skies are gray, and the days are so short they induce melancholy in even the cheeriest of chefs and farmers. Just as locally grown produce is at its most spare, Marco Shaw, chef-owner of Fife in Portland's Beaumont neighborhood, is sitting with his favorite farmer–produce supplier, Shari Surkin of Dancing Roots Farm, to plan for sunnier times.

They're pouring over seed catalogs with all the intensity of children studying a toy catalog before Christmas. Marco chooses the vegetables for the coming year as Shari fills out orders for the seeds. As the weather warms, she'll sow the seeds for unusual vegetables like Gigante kohlrabi, fresh black-eyed peas, and quinoa greens. In addition, she'll get new breeds like "Wrinkle Crinkle" cress and Purple Peacock broccoli (it retains its vibrant purple color when cooked) from her plant breeder and friend, Frank Morton of Wild Garden Seed in Eugene, Oregon. At harvest time Shari will bring the vegetables to Fife's door, just hours out of the ground.

Shari, a former elementary school teacher, values this unique arrangement because, as she puts it, "Looking through the catalogs is fun for both of us; it gets us spurred on to new ideas. There's a learning curve, of course, like the year we tried to grow okra and got only five of them," she says, nudging Marco and laughing, "but we're learning together and every year it gets better."

Shari and her husband, Bryan Dickerson, not only supply vegetables to Fife, they also feed 130 families twenty-six weeks a year with their thriving CSA program. Dancing Roots, their ten-acre farm, lies just above the Sandy River, seventeen miles east of Portland. "That's the great thing about small farms. We can grow so much food for people on so little land, and we do most of the work by hand."

Chef Shaw estimates that approximately 90 percent of the produce he uses comes from Dancing Roots, and the quality of Shari's produce does a lot of the work for him. "Customers say to me all the time, 'That was the best thing I've ever eaten. What did you do to that vegetable?' When I explain that it's just cooked with salt and pepper, that it tastes so good because it's great product, they get really excited because then they figure they might be able to cook it at home. They always want to know where they can find vegetables like that, and I explain they can join Shari's CSA. I've even started to pass out a little printout on how they can get in touch with our suppliers."

But in the winter months buying locally is a challenge for even the most creative cook. "I could write a book on dishes based on kohlrabi and rutabaga alone. You've got to get really creative in January and February," Marco says, laughing. "That's okay, though. My customers understand that I'm committed to buying local food, and when I say local that means no asparagus in January."

The meeting ends with an amiable handshake that serves as their contract: she'll supply him with the best produce she can, and Marco will buy a certain dollar amount of product from her each week, whether it's rutabaga and kale in drizzly January or bushels of heirloom tomatoes and wild blackberries in the heat of summer. Whatever the season, the two have made a symbiotic connection that sustains both all year long, much to the delight of the diners who flock to Fife.

Oysters with Napa Cabbage Slaw

4 to 6 servings

Winter is the best time for fresh oysters. I buy them from Gilson Marine Farms, which brings them from the Oregon coast. If you're planning to buy seafood at the market, bring a little cooler half full of ice to keep the seafood fresh.

I credit the idea of pairing the briny flavor of oysters with crisp Napa cabbage and Asian flavors to Chef Vitaly Paley of Paley's Place. This appetizer was conceived as part of a multicourse prix fixe dinner when I interned there, and the combination of flavors has remained with me ever since.

24 to 36 fresh oysters
2 cups rock salt or chipped ice (optional)
4 Napa cabbage leaves
¼ small carrot, finely julienned
½ green onion, thinly sliced
¼ teaspoon finely minced ginger
½ teaspoon sugar
½ teaspoon rice wine vinegar
1½ teaspoons fish sauce
½ teaspoon high-quality soy sauce
⅛ teaspoon toasted sesame oil
½ teaspoon black sesame seeds (optional)

1. To shuck an oyster, hold it with a thick towel, flat side up, on a flat surface. Push an oyster knife* carefully into the hinge where the shell comes to a point. Wriggle the knife back and forth until the hinge breaks; slide the knife into the oyster, cutting the oyster free from the top shell. Cut the oyster away from the bottom shell, being sure not to spill any oyster liquor in the process. Shuck all of the oysters.
2. Pour rock salt or chipped ice in a serving dish and carefully nestle the oysters in the salt to help keep them upright. (Alternatively, line a serving dish with whole Napa lettuce or leaves.)

continued

3. Cut the tough bottom-most center rib away from the cabbage leaves and discard. Halve the leaves lengthwise, roll them cigar-style, and slice them into thin ribbons. Toss the cabbage, carrot, and green onion in a small bowl. Whisk the ginger, sugar, vinegar, fish sauce, soy sauce, and sesame oil and toss with the cabbage mixture.
4. Mound the slaw on each oyster, sprinkle with black sesame seeds, and serve.

* Oyster knives are short knives with a blunt tip and sturdy handle. They can be found at kitchenware stores.

How to Choose: Oysters should be tightly closed when purchased. Look for oysters that have a deep cup in the bottom shell, which indicates a meaty oyster. If shells are open after purchase, tap the shell; if it quickly snaps shut, the oyster is safe to eat. Discard any oysters that remain open after tapping. Do not store oysters in a sealed plastic bag; the poor guys will suffocate! Instead, refrigerate them covered with a clean, damp cloth for up to 24 hours.

Hazelnut Crab Cakes with Wild Rice

8 to 10 cakes

Patricia Edwards of Linda Brand Crab (see Resources) sells whole Dungeness crabs and lump crabmeat at farmer's markets in Portland, Oregon, nearly year-round. "The peak season is from December through February when there are larger quantities and the crabs are at their most meaty, though the season in Oregon and Washington runs from December through September," says Edwards. Not only is Linda Brand's crab sweet and delicious, but the company also runs a sustainable crabbery by harvesting only full-size male crabs to keep the population healthy. If you don't have access to Linda Brand, use whatever crab is available locally.

½ cup wild rice
¾ cup water
One 2-pound cooked Dungeness crab
2 slices (2 ounces) day-old bread
2 green onions, chopped
1 tablespoon minced Italian parsley
¼ cup hazelnuts, toasted, skinned, and chopped (see instructions, page 146)
⅓ cup mayonnaise
1 teaspoon Old Bay seasoning or crab boil spice blend of your choice
1 egg
Salt and freshly ground black pepper
1 cup all-purpose flour
1 cup vegetable oil

1. Put the rice in a small saucepan with the water, bring to a boil, reduce the heat to maintain a simmer, and cover. Cook until the grains just begin to split, about 40 minutes. Drain and allow to cool slightly.
2. To clean the crab, lift and remove the small tail flap on the white underside of the crab. Lift off the back shell and remove the spongy off-white gills (known as dead man's fingers). Rinse the cavity of all "crab butter" or viscera. Break off the legs and halve the body section. Pick the meat out of the body, crack the legs, remove the meat, and set aside. You should have about 12 ounces of meat.

continued

3. Tear the bread into small pieces and chop by hand or in a food processor into fine crumbs. In a large bowl, combine the crabmeat, ¾ cup of the bread crumbs, rice, green onions, parsley, hazelnuts, mayonnaise, seasoning, and egg. Season with salt and pepper, cover, and refrigerate for at least 1 hour.
4. Preheat the oven to 250°F. Sprinkle the flour on a dinner plate. Gently form the crab mixture into 8 to 10 cakes, about ⅓ cup each (an ice cream scoop works well). If the mixture won't stick together, stir in more bread crumbs a few tablespoons at a time until the mixture can be formed into cakes. Gently dredge the cakes in flour.
5. Heat the oil in a large sauté pan over medium-high heat. Carefully add 4 or 5 cakes and fry them on one side for 4 minutes without moving them. Using 2 spatulas carefully flip them over; cook the second side until crisp and deep brown, about 4 minutes longer, reducing the heat if necessary. Put the cakes on a baking sheet and keep warm in the oven while frying the remaining cakes. Serve with tartar sauce and lemon.

Seared Broccoli and Sweet Onion Salad

4 servings

In this recipe Marco Shaw, chef-owner of Fife in Portland, uses a new hybrid of purple kale and broccoli called Purple Peacock broccoli, but any locally grown broccoli will do. Walla Walla, Maui, and Vidalia sweet onions are the most famous, but other locales, like Hermiston, Oregon, also produce excellent sweets. If they're not available, use shallots. Though Chef Shaw offers this as a warm salad, it can be served as a side dish as well.

1 teaspoon Dijon mustard
1 tablespoon apple cider vinegar
3 tablespoons extra virgin olive oil, divided
1 pound peacock broccoli, cut into ¼-inch-thick spears
1 small (2 cups) sweet onion, sliced into ¼-inch half-moons
8 to 10 fresh sage leaves, roughly chopped
2 ounces soft goat cheese
Salt and freshly ground black pepper

1. Whisk the mustard, vinegar, and 2 tablespoons of the oil in a small bowl. Set aside.
2. Heat a large, heavy-bottomed sauté pan or cast iron skillet over high heat. Pour in the remaining oil, carefully add the broccoli and onions, and sauté until the broccoli turns bright green and is charred in places, about 3 minutes. Add the sage and cook for 1 minute, stirring occasionally with tongs. (Cook the vegetables without overcrowding; you may need to sauté them in 2 batches.)
3. Place the vegetables in a serving bowl and toss with the vinaigrette and cheese. Season with salt and pepper and serve warm.

How to Choose: Choose broccoli that has tight green heads with no yellowing or wilted leaves; refrigerate loosely wrapped in plastic for up to 4 days in the vegetable keeper. Soak organic broccoli in salted lukewarm water for 30 minutes before cooking to remove any insect stowaways.

Golden Beet Salad with Rogue River Blue Cheese and Walnut Vinaigrette

4 servings

This salad is made memorable with blue cheese from the Rogue River Creamery (see Resources). Wheels of this artisan cheese wrapped in Clear Creek Brandy–soaked grape leaves have such stupendous flavor that they have won acclaim at cheese competitions here and abroad. Choose the best artisan blue cheese you can find if Rogue River blue is unavailable.

Walnut oil adds a rich nutty flavor to the dressing; find it in grocery stores among the olive oils. Refrigerate after opening; it will become rancid at room temperature.

8 to 10 ounces (1¼ pounds with greens) small golden beets
1 tablespoon extra virgin olive oil
Salt and freshly ground black pepper
½ cup lukewarm water
2 tablespoons balsamic vinegar
½ teaspoon sugar
1 tablespoon finely minced shallots
3 tablespoons walnut oil*
6 ounces arugula or mixed baby greens
2 ounces Rogue River or other soft blue cheese
½ cup walnuts, toasted

1. Preheat the oven to 400°F. Wash the beets well and remove the greens and stems; reserve for another use. Place the beets in a small baking dish and toss with the olive oil, salt, and pepper. Cover with foil and bake for 40 minutes or until a knife easily goes through the largest beet. Remove the dish from the oven, carefully peel back the foil, and add the water; re-cover and set aside.
2. Combine the vinegar, sugar, and shallots in a small bowl. Gradually whisk in the walnut oil to make an emulsified dressing.

continued

3. When the beets are cool enough to handle, slip off their skins with your fingers and cut them into ½-inch wedges. Toss them with the arugula and enough dressing to coat the salad. Divide the salad among 4 plates, top with dabs of the blue cheese and walnuts, and serve.

* If walnut oil is unavailable, substitute vegetable oil blended with ¼ cup of the toasted walnuts.

How to Choose: Golden beets have a milder flavor than their blood-red counterparts and are a great "gateway" for beet haters. When available, buy beets with the greens still attached and use the tender light green leaves raw in salads and the more mature greens sautéed or steamed with a main course. Look for bunches that have lush green tops with no yellow or brown leaves. Refrigerate beets in the vegetable keeper for weeks; the greens should be used within a few days of purchase. Later in winter, you're more likely to find beets sans greens. Choose small beets for the best texture and flavor.

Grilled Fuyu Persimmons with Frisée and Orange–Brown Butter Dressing

4 servings

In temperate climates you can find orange persimmons in late fall and winter farmer's markets. Their flavor can range from a honeyed pulpyness to a puckery plum-like taste, depending on the variety. Dustin Clark, executive chef at Wildwood, recommends using the small sherbet-orange Fuyu variety in this recipe because it peels easily and can be eaten while it is still firm enough to grill.

Frisée are the tender, pale, frilly leaves of the curly endive plant that have been "blanched" by covering or growing the plants close together to make the leaves more tender. You can also use the pale inner leaves of the less expensive, mature, curly endive (also called chicory).

6 tablespoons butter
3 oranges
1 tablespoon minced shallots
1 teaspoon lemon juice
Salt and freshly ground black pepper
2 ripe Fuyu persimmons
2 teaspoons extra virgin olive oil
6 to 8 ounces frisée, torn into bite-size leaves
¼ cup hazelnuts, toasted, skinned, and chopped (see instructions, page 146)

1. Put the butter in a small sauté pan over medium heat and cook until it begins to brown, swirling the pan occasionally; set aside.
2. Zest 1 of the oranges; set aside the zest. Juice the oranges into a small saucepan and cook over medium heat until reduced to 1 tablespoon of syrupy juice. Add the orange zest, shallots, and lemon juice; stir to combine. Whisk in the butter and season with salt and pepper. Set aside in a warm place.

3. Preheat the grill to medium-high, or heat a grill pan over medium-high heat. Peel and slice the persimmons into ½-inch-thick wedges. Brush them with the oil and grill until lightly charred, about 1 minute per side.
4. Arrange the persimmons on 4 salad plates, mound the frisée on top, drizzle with the orange–brown butter dressing, garnish with the hazelnuts, and serve.

How to Choose: Small, round Fuyu persimmons remain somewhat firm when ripe and have a mild flavor, lending themselves to a quick singe on the grill. The larger Hachiya persimmons have a deep orange skin with a slightly pointed base. They must be eaten when they are extremely ripe and almost pudding-like or they will have an unpleasant puckery tannin kick. When ripe they have a sweet-sour flavor and buttery texture. Persimmons will ripen after purchase if stored in a paper bag with a banana or apple for a few days. Eat them immediately when ripe; they have a narrow window between creamy ripeness and over-matured mush.

Zuppa di Farro

8 servings

This is the perfect solution when you want a big pot of soup on a winter day. It's very adaptable; almost anything in the vegetable keeper can be added. Farro, an ancient grain related to spelt, adds a nutty flavor. Find farro at some grocery stores and by mail order (see Resources).

2 cups dried cannellini beans
10 cups cold water
1 ham bone (optional)
1 bay leaf
3 garlic cloves, peeled
2 teaspoons salt
2 tablespoons olive oil
1 slice pancetta or bacon, chopped
1½ cups chopped onion
1 large carrot, peeled and finely diced
1 small parsnip, peeled and chopped
2 celery stalks, chopped
2 teaspoons chopped fresh sage leaves, or 1 teaspoon dried sage
½ cup dry white wine
1 cup (14 ounces) diced tomatoes in puree
1 cup farro
1 cup 1½-inch cauliflower florets
½ bunch (4 ounces) Lacinato kale
One 4-inch sprig rosemary
Freshly ground black pepper
Grated Parmesan cheese, for garnish

1. Pick through the cannellini beans and rinse well. Put the beans in a large bowl, add enough cold water to cover, and soak for 8 hours or overnight. Drain the beans and transfer them to a large soup pot. Add the water, ham bone, bay leaf, garlic, and salt. Bring to a boil, reduce the heat to maintain a simmer, and cook until the beans still have a little bite, about 30 minutes.
2. Heat a large sauté pan over medium-high heat. Add the oil and pancetta and cook until the pancetta begins to brown, about 5 minutes. Add the onion, carrot, parsnip, celery, and sage. Cook, stirring frequently, until the onion becomes translucent, about 8 minutes. Deglaze the pan with the wine, scraping to loosen any browned bits. Pour the mixture into the beans.
3. Add the tomatoes, farro, and cauliflower to the beans and simmer gently until the beans and farro are tender, about 1 hour.
4. Tear the sturdy ribs and stems away from the kale leaves and discard. Tear the kale into bite-size pieces; add them to the soup and cook for 15 minutes. Add the rosemary to the soup and stir. Steep for 1 minute, then remove the sprig or the flavor will overwhelm the soup. Season with salt and pepper and serve, passing the Parmesan separately. When you store the leftovers, the farro and beans will absorb most of the liquid. Add stock or water when you reheat.

Clam and Smoked Salmon Chowder

6 servings

I visited Seattle for the first time when I was a teenager. My mother and I spent a rainy afternoon at Pike Place Market, and I was fascinated by the fish vendors throwing salmon, the exotic vegetables, and the Asian dumpling vendors. We warmed up with steaming bowls of clam chowder at a restaurant in the market overlooking the Puget Sound. This recipe is an homage to that incredible chowder and that very memorable market experience.

2 slices (4 ounces) thick-cut bacon, finely chopped
1 tablespoon butter
2 cups finely chopped onion
2 celery stalks, chopped
5 tablespoons all-purpose flour
4 cups milk
4 cups Quick Fish Stock (see recipe, page 36) or bottled clam juice
1 bay leaf
1 teaspoon dried sage
1 pound Yukon gold potatoes
1 pound clam meat, chopped
2 ounces smoked salmon, bones and skin removed, chopped
2 tablespoons Italian parsley, finely chopped
Salt and freshly ground black pepper
Hot sauce (optional)

1. Cook the bacon in a large heavy-bottomed soup pot over medium-high heat until the bacon is crisp. Add the butter, onion, and celery and cook, stirring occasionally, until the onion is translucent, about 8 minutes.
2. Reduce the heat to medium and stir in the flour. Cook, stirring constantly, for about 1 minute. Gradually whisk in the milk and stock and bring to a simmer. Add the bay leaf, sage, and potatoes and continue to simmer gently until the potatoes are tender and the soup has thickened, about 20 minutes. Watch the heat closely and stir frequently to prevent scorching.
3. Stir in the clam, salmon, and parsley and cook until just heated through. Season with salt and pepper and serve with warm sourdough bread. Pass hot sauce separately.

Dal with Winter Vegetables

4 to 6 servings

Dal is a thick, satisfying lentil soup that is a staple dish in India. It is easy to make and very adaptable—you can clean out your vegetable keeper and have dinner on the table in less than an hour! Serve with bastmati rice and a simple salad.

1½ cups red lentils
6 cups water
1 bay leaf
One 2-inch cinnamon stick
2 teaspoons salt
1 teaspoon turmeric
2 cups 1-inch cauliflower florets
2 large carrots, peeled and roughly chopped
1 cup roughly chopped cabbage
2 medium (2 cups) Yukon gold potatoes, peeled and cut into 2-inch chunks
3 tablespoons vegetable oil
1 teaspoon brown mustard seeds
1 teaspoon cumin seeds
2 tablespoons peeled, minced ginger
1 tablespoon minced garlic
1 cup finely chopped onion
1 small (2 teaspoons) serrano chile, finely chopped
Salt and freshly ground black pepper
½ cup cilantro, finely chopped

1. Rinse the lentils in a fine-mesh sieve. In a soup pot, bring the lentils, water, bay leaf, cinnamon stick, salt, and turmeric to a boil. Reduce the heat to medium-low and simmer until the lentils have turned a muted amber color and the mixture has become a thick porridge consistency, about 25 minutes.
2. Add the cauliflower, carrots, cabbage, and potatoes and simmer until the potatoes are tender, about 30 minutes.
3. Meanwhile, place a sauté pan over high heat; add the oil and mustard seeds. Cover and cook until the seeds pop, about 30 seconds. Reduce the heat to medium-high and add the cumin seeds, ginger, garlic, onion, and chile. Sauté until the onion begins to brown, about 6 minutes. Stir the mixture into the soup pot, season with salt and pepper, serve in soup bowls, and garnish with the cilantro.

Winter Squash Primer

Winter squash are difficult to sell to today's home cook—there are an ever-growing number of squash varieties appearing at markets, and their consistency in flavor and texture vary. It's all trial and error, but it is a rewarding process, especially if you find a vendor who grows really good, flavorful winter squash.

Just when your local farmer's market is getting ready to end for the winter, pick up a few of the loveliest winter squash you can find (with the stem still attached) and keep them around the house as décor for up to three months before making a meal or two out of them.

1. **NEW JERSEY CHEESE OR CHEESE PUMPKIN:** This beautiful squash looks like a slightly flattened jack-o-lantern painted flat beige. The sweet orange flesh makes great soup, risotto, or tortellini filling.

2. **JARRAHDALE:** The tough skin ranges from spruce to powdery green (later in the season) with deep orange flesh that cooks to a silky, creamy texture. It can be bland; roasting and pairing with flavorful ingredients or adding to sugary dessert custards or pies is best.

3. **ROUGE VIF D'ETAMPES:** The prettiest of the bunch, the Cinderella pumpkin is usually very large with tough, bright red-orange skin. The flesh is moist and varies from a definite pumpkin flavor to simply bland. It is best roasted and added to risotto or dishes with bold flavors.

4. **RED KURI:** This pretty squash has a crimson-orange skin and an elegant round shape that comes to a slight point on the stem end. The tough skin yields to smooth, dry flesh with a chestnut-like flavor similar to Kabocha squash. It's good for creamy soups and curries.

5. **KABOCHA:** This squat, dark green squash has a thick skin, light orange flesh, and a dry texture similar to chestnuts when cooked. Kabocha is a good option for curries because it holds its shape when cooked.

6. **BLUE HUBBARD:** This large, round squash comes to point at the blossom end. The thick, matte, gray-green skin hides a brilliant orange flesh that is often sweet and a bit watery. Because of their size, it's common to see them for sale cut up in manageable pieces. They're good for pies, soups with strong seasoning like curry powder, and tortellini filling. The Golden Hubbard has similar characteristics.

7. **DELICATA:** This small squash sports a delicate yellow skin with green and orange stripes. Delicatas are wonderful halved and stuffed with wild rice stuffing or peeled and added to roasted root vegetables. They spoil quickly if the skin has any nicks, so choose them carefully and refrigerate after purchase.

8. **SWEET DUMPLING:** This little squash has cream-colored skin and ivy green stripes. With a few weeks of storage, it turns a golden yellow with orange stripes. The pale yellow flesh is starchy with a sweet, corn-like flavor. Its size makes it ideal for roasting and stuffing. You can also roast wedges and serve as a side dish—the skin is edible.

Cinderella Pumpkin Risotto with Fried Sage

4 servings

Risotto is a good excuse to stand next to a warm stove, sip some wine, and stare into space while you methodically stir—consider it a little getaway, if only for 18 minutes. Try different squashes; the crimson orange squash I use (aka Cinderella squash) has great pumpkin flavor, but almost any winter squash will do.

One 6-pound Rouge Vif D'Etampes squash
4 tablespoons mild-flavored olive oil, divided
Salt and freshly ground black pepper
6½ cups vegetable or chicken stock
½ cup sage leaves, rinsed and patted dry
1 cup finely chopped onion
1½ cups Arborio or Vialone Nano rice
½ cup dry white wine or vermouth
2 tablespoons butter
½ cup grated Parmesan cheese

1. Preheat the oven to 425°F and line a baking sheet with parchment paper. Cover a cutting board with a clean dish towel.
2. With a fork, prick the top of the squash several times and microwave for 3 minutes for easier cutting. (Alternatively, bake in a preheated oven until slightly softened, about 10 minutes.) Set the squash on the towel to prevent it from slipping and push the tip of a sharp chef's knife into the squash near the stem. Carefully push the knife to the bottom of the squash. If the knife sticks, *do not* attempt to pull it out. Tap the handle with a rubber mallet or meat tenderizer until the knife sinks through the squash. Rotate the squash and cut through the other side the same way. Push the halves apart with your hands; with a paring knife or soup-spoon scrape the seeds and stringy bits away from the flesh and discard. Tightly wrap half the squash in plastic wrap and reserve for another use. (Alternatively, after preparing the risotto, peel, dice, and freeze the reserved squash.)

3. Halve the remaining squash and put half on the prepared baking sheet. Peel the other half and cut into ½-inch dice. Place the diced squash on the baking sheet and toss with 2 tablespoons of the oil, salt, and pepper. Bake until the diced squash is tender, about 25 minutes. Remove the diced squash and set aside. Turn over the unpeeled squash and continue to roast until it is tender, about 50 minutes longer. Scoop out the flesh, mash slightly, and set aside (you should have 2 cups).
4. In a medium saucepan, bring the stock to a gentle simmer.
5. In a large saucepan, over medium-high heat, heat the remaining oil until hot but not smoking. Carefully add the sage leaves and fry until they are golden brown, about 1 minute. Remove the leaves with a slotted spoon and drain on paper towels.
6. Add the onion to the oil and cook until it is translucent, about 8 minutes. Stir in the rice and cook for 1 minute. Add the wine and stir constantly with a wooden spoon until the liquid is absorbed, about 1 minute. Add a few ladles of the warm stock and a few spoonfuls of the mashed squash; bring to a simmer, stirring constantly. When the rice no longer looks soupy, add a few more ladles of stock and mashed squash. Continue adding and stirring until the rice is tender with a slight chew, about 18 minutes. You may not need all the stock. The rice will thicken as soon as you take it off the heat; add the remaining liquid if you prefer the risotto saucier.
7. Gently fold in the diced squash, butter, and Parmesan, and season with salt and pepper. Divide among 4 bowls, top with sage leaves, and serve.

Twice-Baked Irish Potatoes with Stout Onions and Kale

4 servings

"What's your favorite potato story?" Gene Theil, the spunky potato farmer, asked me one crisp morning as I chose from his russets. I drew a blank. "Everyone has a potato story," he assured me. It finally dawned on me: colcannon. My grandmother used to make the satisfying mash of kale or cabbage and potatoes for me when I was a kid. She said its origins came from necessity when times were tough in Ireland. Women would add kale, cabbage, or even seaweed to their mashed potatoes to stretch the meager harvest—the greener the colcannon, the tougher the times.

My love of simple but comforting colcannon inspired this satisfying variation of double-stuffed potatoes; it's a sort of Irish soul food, if you will.

- 4 large (8 to 10 ounces each) russet potatoes, scrubbed
- 1 tablespoon plus 1 teaspoon olive oil, divided
- 2 medium (3 cups) onions, thinly sliced
- 1 cup Irish-style stout
- ½ bunch (3 ounces) lacinato kale or Russian kale
- 1 cup buttermilk
- 2 tablespoons butter, at room temperature
- ½ teaspoon mustard powder
- Salt and freshly ground black pepper
- 1 cup grated cheddar cheese

1. Preheat the oven to 400°F. Rub the potatoes with 1 teaspoon of the oil and place directly on the oven rack. Bake until they squish easily when gently squeezed, 45 minutes to 1 hour.
2. Heat the remaining oil in a large sauté pan over medium heat. Add the onions and cook, stirring frequently, until they begin to brown, about 15 minutes. Add a splash of the stout and scrape up any browned bits. Continue to cook, occasionally deglazing the pan with the stout until the onions are deep brown and all the stout is used, about 45 minutes total.
3. Tear the tough ribs and stems away from the kale and discard. Roughly chop the leaves and add half the kale to the onions, tossing with tongs to wilt the leaves. Add the remaining kale, toss, cover, and cook until tender, about 5 minutes. Remove from the heat.
4. With a serrated knife, slice off the top quarter of each potato. Use a soupspoon to scoop out the flesh, leaving a ¼-inch-thick shell on the bottom and sides. Mash the flesh with the buttermilk, butter, and mustard powder. Gently fold in the onion-kale mixture and season with salt and pepper. Mound the mixture into the potato shells, sprinkle the tops with the cheese, and place on a baking sheet. Bake until the cheese is melted, about 20 minutes, and serve warm as a side dish or a vegetarian main course.

Handcut Angel Hair Pasta with Black Truffle Butter (Tajarìn con Burro di Tartufi Neri)

6 side dish or appetizer servings

I am lucky enough to live in Oregon, where both black and white truffles grow in the wild. My love of this wild, aromatic fungus began when I helped out during truffle season at Antica Torre, a family-owned restaurant in Piedmont, Italy. When I asked Cinto Albarello, the patriarch of the Antica Torre clan, how to describe the flavor of local white truffles, he said, "There are no words." Indeed.

Truffles are commonly called black gold and can fetch from $50 to $500 per pound, depending on their size and quality. The egg yolk pasta in this recipe highlights the flavor and aroma of the truffles. If you're unable to find fresh truffles, use a well-made truffle-infused oil instead (see Resources).

3½ cups all-purpose flour, divided
1 pinch salt
8 large egg yolks, whisked
½ ounce black truffle, or 1 to 2 tablespoons truffle oil
½ cup (1 stick) butter, at room temperature
1 cup grated Parmesan cheese
Salt and freshly ground black pepper

1. Put 2½ cups of the flour and salt in the bowl of an electric mixer. Gradually add the egg yolks while blending on low speed with the paddle attachment. Add water 1 tablespoon at a time (up to 4 tablespoons) to create a stiff dough. Switch to the dough hook and knead on low speed for 3 minutes; the dough will be dry and very stiff. Hold the mixer while it is kneading to steady it.
2. To mix by hand, pour the flour and salt directly onto a cutting board, form a well in the center, and add the egg yolks. Mix gently with your hands, adding water 1 tablespoon at a time (up to 4 tablespoons) until the dough comes together; knead until smooth and elastic, about 10 minutes.
3. Divide the dough into 4 discs, cover with plastic wrap, and let rest for 30 minutes. Dust a baking sheet with some of the remaining flour.

▸ *continued*

4. Roll 1 dough disc on a pasta machine (following manufacturer's instructions) until it is as thin as possible, cutting the sheets into 6-inch lengths to make them more manageable. Dust 1 pasta length with flour and roll it cigar-style. Slice the roll as thinly as possible with a sharp knife. Lift the pasta coils with your fingers, tossing and fluffing with a little flour to unravel the pasta into long, thin ribbons. Place the cut pasta on the prepared baking sheet. Repeat with the remaining dough.
5. To clean the truffle, carefully brush off any dirt with a moistened baby toothbrush (it will retain its black exterior). Thinly shave the truffle with a knife or sharp vegetable peeler and set aside. Melt the butter in a large sauté pan over medium heat until bubbly, add the truffle, and swirl to combine. If using truffle oil, add it to the pan now. Turn off the heat and keep in a warm place.
6. Bring a large pot of salted water to a boil. Add half the pasta and cook until al dente, 30 seconds to 1 minute. With a fine-mesh sieve, quickly scoop out the pasta, shake off the excess water, and place the pasta in the butter-truffle pan.
7. Gently toss the pasta, add the Parmesan, and season with salt and pepper. Transfer to warm bowls and serve.

How to Choose: To purchase the best truffle, bring it close to your nose. It will be very aromatic and have a slight give when gently squeezed with your fingertips. If it doesn't have much aroma, it's immature. Ripen in the refrigerator in a small airtight glass container or wrapped in an unbleached paper towel and placed in a paper bag. Check each day and use when it exudes a buttery, musky aroma—it can take several days to ripen. Never buy or use a truffle with a foul ammonia or dung-like aroma, or one that is overly squishy. White truffles have the same indicators of ripeness but are usually eaten raw; cooking them will kill their delicate aroma.

Petrale Sole with Smoked Mussels Hash and Horseradish Vinaigrette

4 servings

Wildwood has been famous for its market-driven cuisine since it opened in 1994. It has become a leader in the Pacific Northwest's farm-to-table culinary revolution, staying closely tied to the farmers and purveyors of the area. This dish is adapted from a recipe by Chef Dustin Clark. Petrale sole, smoked mussels (available at fish markets where smoked salmon is sold), apples, and potatoes celebrate the comforting flavors of winter in a creative way.

1 tablespoon champagne or white wine vinegar
1½ teaspoons prepared horseradish
Juice and zest of ½ lemon
¼ cup crème fraîche or sour cream
6 tablespoons olive oil, divided
Salt and freshly ground black pepper
3 large (1½ pounds) Yukon gold potatoes, whole and unpeeled
2 large (1½ cups) Braeburn apples, peeled, cored, and diced
1 tablespoon fresh thyme leaves, chopped
6 ounces smoked mussels, roughly chopped if large
Four 6-ounce petrale sole fillets
Flour, for dredging

1. Preheat the oven to 375°F.
2. Whisk the vinegar, horseradish, lemon juice, lemon zest, crème fraîche, and 2 tablespoons of the oil in a small bowl. Season with salt and pepper and set aside.
3. Place the potatoes in a saucepan, cover with cold water, and season the water liberally with salt. Bring to a boil, reduce the heat, and simmer until the potatoes are tender when pierced with a paring knife, about 30 minutes. Drain; when cool enough to handle, slip off the skins and cut the potatoes into bite-size pieces.

4. Heat 2 tablespoons of the oil in a large sauté pan over medium-high heat until hot. Add the potatoes, apples, and thyme; cook without stirring until the potatoes are golden brown on the bottom, about 5 minutes. Using a spatula, turn hash over in sections and cook for an additional 5 minutes, or until golden brown. Fold in the smoked mussels, reduce the heat to low, and keep warm.
5. Pat the fillets dry, season sparingly with salt on both sides, and allow them to sit for 1 minute. Heat the remaining oil in a medium sauté pan over medium-high heat. Dredge each fillet in flour, shaking off the excess. Working in 2 batches, sear the fillets until golden brown, about 3 minutes per side.
6. Divide the potato mixture among 4 plates and top each with a fish fillet. Drizzle with the horseradish vinaigrette and serve.

Mussels with Chorizo and Rouille

4 servings

Chef Jason Owens of Simpatica Catering and Dining Hall uses chorizo from his butcher shop, Viande Meats, for this spicy take on Pacific Northwest wine-steamed mussels. Find chorizo in most Mexican markets or grocery stores, or at your farmer's market sausage vendor. Chef Owens encourages you to roll up your sleeves and get messy. He says, "Serve the mussels communally right out of the pan with grilled bread to sop up the broth. It's the best part."

2 tablespoons olive oil

1 medium yellow onion, julienned lengthwise from root end through tip

¾ pound chorizo sausage, casings removed

2 pounds mussels, scrubbed and de-bearded

Salt and freshly ground black pepper

1 cup dry white wine

2⅓ cups rouille (see recipe, page 192)

1 loaf rustic bread, sliced and grilled

1. Heat the oil in a heavy-bottomed sauté pan or large cast iron skillet over medium heat. Add the onion and cook, stirring constantly, until it is well caramelized, about 10 minutes. (Reduce the heat and add a few tablespoons of water if the onion begins to burn.)
2. Add the chorizo; while it is cooking break the chunks with a wooden spoon. Cook until it is well browned. Drain the fat.
3. Return the pan to the heat, increase the heat to medium-high, and add the mussels. Season with salt and pepper and cook for 1 minute. Add the wine and stir gently. Cover, bring to a boil, and cook until the mussels open, 2 to 3 minutes. Discard mussels that do not open.
4. Serve the mussels from the pan, passing the rouille and bread separately.

How to Choose: Mussels are best in the colder months of late fall, winter, and early spring. The shells should be tightly closed or should clamp shut when tapped. Avoid mussels that stay open or those with broken shells. Refrigerate mussels in a shallow bowl covered with a damp towel and use within 2 days of purchase. Leave the hairy beards protruding from the sides of the shells on, pulling them off the mussels right before cooking. Mussel size does not indicate quality; it's simply a matter of personal preference—some folks relish big, meaty specimens, while others prefer the delicate texture of smaller mussels.

Rouille

2⅓ cups

Rouille ("rust" in French) is a rich, smoky sauce commonly served with bouillabaisse, the famous fish stew from the south of France. Leftover rouille makes a wonderful sandwich spread, vegetable dip, or accompaniment for chicken or grilled fish; refrigerate in an airtight container for up to 3 weeks.

1 cup roasted red bell peppers (see recipe, page 75), roughly chopped
1 egg yolk
2 teaspoons finely chopped garlic
½ teaspoon red wine vinegar
2 heaping tablespoons hazelnuts, toasted and skinned (see instructions, page 146)
1 cup extra virgin olive oil
Salt and freshly ground black pepper
Juice from ¼ lemon

1. Puree the bell peppers, egg yolk, garlic, vinegar, and hazelnuts in a food processor until smooth. With the machine running, add the oil in a slow, steady stream. The sauce will thicken as you add the oil.
2. Season with salt, pepper, and a squeeze of lemon juice.

Goat Cheese Ravioli with Roasted Red Pepper Sauce

4 to 6 servings

At The Farm Café, Chef Fearn Smith makes this dish using locally made fresh pasta sheets. I've included an easy pasta dough recipe so you can make fresh pasta at home. You can also make the ravioli with fresh wonton wrappers, though the results won't be as wonderful. Chef Smith uses soft, mild goat cheese from Fraga Farms (see Resources), available at Portland-area farmer's markets and grocery stores. Experiment with soft goat cheeses from your local market to find one that suits your taste.

FOR THE RAVIOLI:

1 pound fresh pasta dough (see recipe, page 195)
8 ounces fresh Fraga Farms goat cheese
¼ cup grated Parmesan cheese
¼ cup grated Pecorino Romano or other hard sheep's milk cheese
¼ cup ricotta or soft farmer's cheese
¼ cup hazelnuts, toasted, skinned, and minced (see instructions, page 146)
½ cup fresh basil leaves (optional)
1 egg, beaten

FOR THE RED PEPPER SAUCE:

2 cups roasted red bell peppers (see recipe, page 75)
2 tablespoons extra virgin olive oil
1 teaspoon lemon juice
2 teaspoons good-quality balsamic vinegar
2 tablespoons warm water
Cayenne pepper
Salt and freshly ground black pepper
Chopped Italian parsley, for garnish

1. Prepare the pasta dough and set aside. Lightly flour a baking sheet and set aside.
2. Combine the cheeses and hazelnuts in a medium mixing bowl.
3. On a cutting board, lay the basil leaves in a stack with the stem ends toward you. Roll the leaves cigar-style and thinly slice them into ribbons. Add to the cheese mixture.

▶ *continued*

4. Lay a long pasta sheet on a lightly floured work surface and cut crosswise into 2 strips of equal length. Place rounded tablespoons of the cheese mixture on 1 piece of pasta, spacing the mounds 3 inches apart. Brush the egg around the mounds and top with the second piece of pasta. Gently press around the cheese mounds to seal, pushing out any air bubbles that are trapped between the 2 layers of pasta.
5. Using a pastry cutter or sharp paring knife, cut the filled dough into 3- by 3-inch squares. Place the ravioli on the prepared baking sheet as you work. Pasta scraps can be added to the unrolled pasta and used again. (Ravioli can be made ahead to this point. Freeze ravioli on a parchment paper–lined baking sheet until firm, then store in sealable plastic bags until ready to use. Cook from the frozen state.)
6. To prepare the sauce, in a blender mix the bell peppers, oil, lemon juice, vinegar, and water until smooth. Season with the cayenne pepper, salt, and pepper to taste. Transfer the sauce to a small saucepan and gently warm over medium-low heat.
7. Bring a large pot of salted water to a *gentle* boil. Gently drop the ravioli into the water, allowing 6 to 8 ravioli per person. (You may have to cook the ravioli in batches to avoid overcrowding.) Cook until the ravioli float to the surface and the pasta is tender, about 3 minutes. (Cut off a corner of the pasta and taste to determine doneness.) Using a slotted spoon, remove the ravioli and divide among pasta bowls. Top with the warm sauce and parsley and serve.

Pasta Dough for Ravioli

1 pound, enough for 60 ravioli

2 cups all-purpose flour
3 eggs, lightly beaten
2 pinches salt

1. Blend the flour, eggs, and salt in the bowl of an electric mixer with the paddle attachment until the dough just comes together. Switch to the dough hook and knead on low speed for 5 minutes. (Alternatively, mix ingredients together with a spoon and knead by hand for 10 minutes on a lightly floured board.) Wrap the dough in plastic wrap and allow it to rest for 30 minutes.
2. Divide the dough into 4 pieces. Flatten 1 piece slightly and feed it through the pasta maker on the thickest setting. It may look a little raggedy. Fold the ends into the center as if folding a letter and feed the pasta through the machine again. Dust the pasta sheet with flour and continue to feed through the rollers, turning to the next-thinnest setting each time through until you reach the second-thinnest setting. Cut the sheets into manageable lengths as you work. Use the finished dough to prepare ravioli.

Spice-Crusted Lamb Chops with Quince

2 servings

Quince are an ancient winter fruit Europeans use in cakes, jams, and breads. In the Middle East quince are often part of sweet-savory dishes like this recipe. The aroma of ripe quince combines jasmine flowers, ripe apples, and passion fruit. Resist the urge to chomp into the fruit; they have an unpleasant astringent quality when uncooked. Cooked, they become a sweet, rosy-hued fruit that makes everything from cakes to stew taste exotic and delicious.

½ cup sugar
1 cup water
2 medium (about 12 ounces) ripe quince, peeled and cored
1 clove
1 bay leaf
½ teaspoon ground cumin
½ teaspoon ground coriander
1 pinch cayenne pepper
½ teaspoon ground cinnamon
1 teaspoon kosher salt
½ teaspoon freshly ground black pepper
1½ pounds (about 4 to 6) lamb rib chops
1 tablespoon vegetable oil
1 tablespoon cold butter
1 cup ruby port wine
½ cup chicken stock

1. Combine the sugar and water in a small saucepan; stir to dissolve. Slice the quince ½ inch thick and add to the pan with the clove and bay leaf. Cover and simmer over medium heat, stirring occasionally, until the quince is just tender, 25 to 30 minutes. Remove the fruit with a slotted spoon and set aside. Increase the heat to medium-high, and cook until the liquid thickens and is reduced to about ¼ cup. Remove from the heat and set aside.
2. Meanwhile, on a plate, combine the cumin, coriander, cayenne pepper, cinnamon, salt, and black pepper. Coat the chops with the spice mixture; discard any excess spice mixture.

▸ *continued*

3. Turn on the kitchen exhaust or open a window. Put a heavy-bottomed sauté pan or cast iron skillet over high heat and heat the oil until hot but not smoking. Carefully add the chops, reduce the heat to medium-high, and sear on each side for 2½ minutes for medium rare or until an instant-read thermometer inserted into the center of the thickest chop registers 135°F. Remove the chops from the pan and cover loosely with foil.
4. Wipe out the sauté pan with a paper towel. Add the butter and quince to the pan and cook until the quince begin to caramelize, about 2 minutes. Remove pan from heat, add the reserved cooking liquid, pour the mixture over the chops, and replace the foil.
5. Deglaze the sauté pan with the wine, scraping up browned bits from the bottom. Add the stock, bring to a rolling boil, and cook until reduced by half, about 4 minutes. Season with salt and pepper and divide between 2 deep plates. Arrange the chops and quince on top and serve.

How to Choose: Quince are available from late fall until January or February. Choose firm quince with pale yellow skin and a heady fragrance. Refrigerate loosely wrapped in plastic for up to 1 week. Green quince are not ready to use but can be ripened at room temperature until their skins turn bright yellow and their aroma fills the room. Some more fragrant varieties sport a downy fuzz that peels off easily.

Beef and All of the Beet Borscht

8 servings

I use the grating disc on my food processor to prepare the beets so I don't stain my fingers, cutting board, and countertop with beet juice. Dice the beets if you prefer chunkier borscht. If the beets you buy still have the greens attached, add them to the soup for additional flavor and vitamins.

2 pounds boneless beef chuck, trimmed of fat, cut into 1-inch cubes
Salt and freshly ground black pepper
3 to 4 tablespoons vegetable oil, divided
1/2 cup flour
2 tablespoons tomato paste
6 cups water or beef stock
1 bay leaf
1 bunch (1 1/2 pounds) red beets, greens attached
1 large carrot, peeled
1 medium (4 ounces) turnip, peeled
1 1/2 cups finely chopped onion
1/4 teaspoon ground allspice
2 teaspoons dried dill
2 tablespoons red wine vinegar
Sour cream, for garnish

1. Season the beef generously with salt and pepper. Heat 1 tablespoon of the oil in a large soup pot over medium-high heat. Dredge a handful of meat in the flour, shake off the excess, and add to the pot. Cook until the meat is brown on one side, turn, and continue to cook until the second side is brown, about 2 minutes. Reduce the heat if the flour begins to burn. Remove the meat and repeat with the remaining beef, adding oil as needed.
2. Pour out any oil remaining, return the beef to the pot, and stir in the tomato paste. Cook until the tomato paste begins to color, about 30 seconds. Add the water and bay leaf and bring to a gentle simmer over medium heat.
3. Meanwhile, separate the beets from their greens. Peel the beets under cold running water and grate them in a food processor. Grate the carrot, turnip, and onion. (Alternatively, finely chop the vegetables.) Add the grated vegetables, allspice, and dill to the pot. Cover and gently simmer until the beef is tender, about 3 hours.
4. Wash the beet greens well, remove the tough stems, and finely chop the leaves. Stir them into the borscht and simmer for 15 minutes.
5. Taste the soup and add salt and vinegar to taste. Serve with sour cream and warm bread.

Sage-Braised Pork Shoulder with Herb Spaetzle

6 to 8 servings

Pork shoulder, also called Boston butt or picnic ham, is the inexpensive upper part of the foreleg. The flavor of pork shoulder is much richer than leaner loin cuts, and the meat cooks down to a roast that nearly melts in your mouth. Most meat vendors at farmer's markets are eager to sell you the shoulder cut; it's usually passed over for the leaner loin and loin chop cuts. When choosing a pork shoulder, Chef Ben Stenn of Celilo Restaurant and Bar advises, "Make sure the roast has a good layer of fat on it; it helps insulate the meat while it cooks." Chef Stenn pairs his sage-infused pork shoulder with little poached German dumplings called spaetzle. Braised red cabbage is a nice accompaniment.

1 tablespoon olive oil
One 3- to 4-pound pork shoulder roast
Salt and freshly ground black pepper
1 cup roughly chopped onion
1 stalk celery, roughly chopped
1 large carrot, peeled and roughly chopped
1 cup dry white wine
10 black peppercorns
1 bay leaf
1 cup fresh sage leaves
4 to 6 cups chicken stock
4 cups Herb Spaetzle (see recipe, page 202)

1. Preheat the oven to 350°F. Heat the oil in a large cast iron pot or Dutch oven over medium-high heat. Season the roast with salt and pepper and sear it on all sides until well browned. Remove from the pan and drain all but 1 tablespoon of fat.
2. Add the onion, celery, and carrot and cook, stirring occasionally, until the vegetables begin to brown. Increase the heat to high and deglaze the pan with the wine, scraping up any browned bits with a wooden spoon. Boil until reduced by half, about 5 minutes.

3. Add the peppercorns, bay leaf, and sage, and nestle the roast on top of the vegetables. Add enough stock to come halfway up the sides of the roast and bring to a simmer over high heat.
4. Transfer the pot to the oven and bake, turning over the roast with tongs every 40 minutes until the meat is very tender and almost falling apart, 3½ to 4 hours. (The roast can be cooked ahead to this point and refrigerated for up to 2 days. Remove the fat that has risen to the top of the braising liquid before reheating.)
5. Ladle the braising liquid out of the pan and strain it through a fine-mesh sieve into a medium saucepan. Reduce the oven temperature to 250°F, cover the roast with foil, and return it to the oven.
6. Put the saucepan over high heat and boil until the liquid is thick and glossy, 30 to 40 minutes, spooning off any fat that rises to the surface. Season with salt and pepper, or thin slightly with water if the braising liquid is too salty.
7. Prepare the spaetzle and set aside.
8. Slice the roast into thick slices or chunks and serve with the braising liquid and spaetzle. The flavor of the roast improves with time, so try preparing it a few days in advance if possible and reheating it in the braising liquid before carving and serving.

Herb Spaetzle

6 to 8 side dish servings

Spaetzle makers are available at specialty shops, or you can press the batter through the holes of a large-holed colander (¼ inch or larger), food mill, or coarse cheese grater to make the irregularly shaped dumplings.

3 eggs
¾ cup milk
1 teaspoon salt
¼ teaspoon black pepper
1 tablespoon minced mixed fresh winter herbs (thyme, rosemary, sage)
2¼ cups flour
2 tablespoons butter

1. Whisk the eggs, milk, salt, pepper, and herbs in a medium bowl. Sift the flour over the mixture and stir with a wooden spoon until smooth and thick.
2. Bring a large pot of salted water to a simmer. Hold the spaetzle maker over the water, add ¼ of the batter, and scrape it back and forth, forcing little bits of batter into the simmering water. Remove the bits with a slotted spoon as they float to the top, transfer them to a sauté pan with the butter, and keep them warm over low heat while continuing to cook the remaining batter.
3. When all the batter is cooked and in the sauté pan, raise the heat to high, briefly toast the spaetzle in the butter until golden brown, and serve.

Braised Red Cabbage with Caraway Seeds

8 side dish servings

A natural complement to hearty winter dishes, braised red cabbage is the ultimate cold-weather comfort food. Add peeled apple wedges to the pan to sweeten the dish, if you like. This recipe can easily be halved. You can make the recipe vegetarian by replacing the bacon with 4 teaspoons of vegetable oil.

2 slices thick-cut bacon, cut into ½-inch pieces
1 medium onion, thinly sliced
One 2½-pound head red cabbage (12 cups sliced)
2 teaspoons caraway seeds
¼ cup red wine vinegar
¼ cup chicken stock or water
1 heaping tablespoon brown sugar
Salt and freshly ground black pepper

1. Heat a large sauté pan over medium heat. Sauté the bacon until the fat renders and the bacon begins to crisp. Add the onion and cook until it becomes translucent, about 8 minutes.
2. Meanwhile, carefully halve the cabbage using a sharp chef's knife. Cut each half into 2 pieces and cut away the tough white core in the center of each piece. Thinly slice the cabbage.
3. Increase the heat to medium high and add a few handfuls of cabbage to the pan; stir with tongs and cover. Cook until the cabbage is slightly wilted, about 2 minutes. Continue adding cabbage and wilting until all the cabbage will fit in the pan.
4. Add the caraway seeds, vinegar, stock, brown sugar, salt, and pepper. Cover, reduce the heat to medium, and cook, stirring occasionally, until the cabbage is tender, about 30 minutes. The cabbage can be kept warm over low heat for up to 1 hour before serving.

Celery Root Mashed Potatoes

6 to 8 servings

Celery root (also called celeriac), with its gnarly roots and a dull beige skin, hardly beckons you to wrestle with it. But when you get past the exterior, you will find a crisp ivory vegetable with a clean, celery-like taste. Celery root is delicious raw when tossed with a tangy mayonnaise-based dressing or cooked in purees and stews. Here, it makes mashed potatoes memorable.

3 pounds (about 6 large) Yukon gold potatoes, peeled and cut into 2-inch chunks
1 to 1½ pounds celery root
3 medium garlic cloves, peeled
1 tablespoon kosher salt
1½ cups whole milk
1 bay leaf
4 black peppercorns
3 tablespoons butter, at room temperature
¼ teaspoon ground nutmeg
2 pinches cayenne pepper
Freshly ground black pepper

1. Put the potatoes in a large pot with enough cold water to cover. Slice off the top stalks (if present) and bottom roots from the celery root and peel the skin and hairy roots away with a sharp vegetable peeler or paring knife. Cut the celery root into ½-inch slabs, then into 2-inch-long sticks; add to the pot. Add the garlic, salt, and additional cold water to cover the vegetables by 2 inches. Bring to a boil over high heat and cook until a paring knife slices easily through the largest piece of potato, about 40 minutes.
2. Meanwhile, heat the milk, bay leaf, and peppercorns in a small saucepan over low heat.

3. Drain the potatoes and celery root. Force them through a potato ricer or food mill to make a silky-smooth puree. (Alternatively, mash the vegetables with a potato masher until lumps are gone.)
4. Stir in the butter, nutmeg, and cayenne pepper. Remove the bay leaf and peppercorns from the warm milk with a slotted spoon. Add enough milk to potatoes to make a loose puree. Season with salt and black pepper and serve warm.

How to Choose: Celery root is best from fall to early spring. Look for a root about the size of a small softball with shallow crevices and minimal roots at the bottom end. The freshest have green stalks still attached. If the root has been trimmed of its stalks, inspect the top—it should not be mushy or brown. Don't buy very large roots that feel light compared to smaller ones; they will be spongy in the center. To stop the flesh from oxidizing, put the root in cooking liquid or a dressing with some acidity within 5 minutes of paring. Store in the vegetable keeper unwashed in a paper bag for up to 2 weeks.

Braised Lacinato Kale

4 servings

Lacinato kale has dark green, almost black leaves with a crinkled texture (it's sometimes called dinosaur kale for its reptilian appearance) and a deep, satisfying flavor similar to chard. This recipe works well with turnip, collard, and beet greens as well; adjust the amount of liquid you add and the time you steam-cook the greens, which depends on the tenderness of the leaves. Collards can take as long as 20 minutes to steam; beet greens are done in about 3 minutes.

When raw, greens look like a mountain of food, but they wilt considerably when heat is applied. In this recipe I call for two bunches of kale for four people as a side dish, but I can eat one bunch all by myself, especially if it's poured over warm cornbread. The recipe can be made vegetarian by omitting the bacon; sauté kale in 1 tablespoon of olive oil instead.

2 bunches lacinato kale
1 slice thick-cut bacon, roughly chopped
1 tablespoon red wine vinegar
3 tablespoons chicken stock
1 generous pinch sugar
Salt and freshly ground black pepper

1. Rinse the kale well and tear the leaves from the tough rib that runs up the center of each leaf. Tear the leaves into 2-inch pieces and place in a colander.
2. Cook the bacon in a large saucepan over medium-high heat until crisp; with a slotted spoon, transfer it to a small bowl, leaving the bacon fat in the pan.
3. Put the leaves with water still clinging to them in the pan; stir with tongs to wilt them. Add the vinegar, stock, and sugar. Cover and cook over medium heat, stirring occasionally, until the leaves are tender, about 10 minutes. Season with salt and pepper, sprinkle the bacon over the top, and serve.

How to Choose: Lacinato kale comes in bunches of about 12 leaves. Look for tender, relatively small leaves, 2 to 3 inches wide. Avoid kale that feels limp or has yellowing leaves. The longer kale sits, the more cabbagey it will taste and smell; for best results use it within 3 days.

Maple-Glazed Turnips and Carrots

4 servings

Turnips are not well loved, thanks to the old-fashioned treatment of long storage and boiling mercilessly. When young turnips are briefly steamed or sautéed, they are quite mild and tasty. Be sure to use them quickly—they attain an acrid flavor as they age. The freshest turnips come with the greens still attached; the greens do well sautéed as in Braised Lacinato Kale (see recipe, opposite).

12 ounces young turnips, 2 inches or less in diameter
1 large carrot, peeled
¼ cup chicken stock or water
2 tablespoons butter
1 tablespoon grade A or B maple syrup
Salt and freshly ground black pepper

1. Scrub and peel the turnips and cut into quarters or sixths, depending on their size. Slice the carrot at an angle into ½-inch-thick pieces.
2. Put the vegetables and stock in a medium saucepan and bring to a boil. Cover and cook until the turnips are barely tender, about 7 minutes. Reduce the heat to medium-high and add the butter and maple syrup. Stir to coat the vegetables and continue to cook uncovered until the vegetables are glazed and beginning to caramelize around the edges, about 2 minutes. Season with salt and pepper and serve.

How to Choose: Many types of turnips are available, from the standard purple-topped supermarket variety to specialty turnips like the delicious Golden Globe and the small, stark-white Tokyo. For the mildest flavor, choose turnips that were recently harvested. If the greens are still attached, you can better gauge their freshness—fresh green leaves means a fresh turnip. Buy small turnips, no larger than 2 inches in diameter, that are firm and not spongy. Though they are available all year, turnips are best in cold, damp weather; avoid them when the weather is hot or dry.

Wild Rice and Dried Cherry Stuffing

6 to 8 side dish servings

This moist stuffing is ideal as a side dish for chicken or turkey, or stuffed into delicata squash. Unsweetened cherries vary in quality, from almost flavorless shrivels to the delicious, fruity Bings I buy from Cherry Country (see Resources), a vendor at my farmer's market.

4 cups water
1 cup wild rice
1½ teaspoons salt, divided
¼ cup olive oil
1 cup finely chopped onion
2 stalks celery, finely chopped
1 Gala apple, cored, peeled, and finely chopped
2 tablespoons poultry seasoning
¼ cup Italian parsley leaves, minced
1¼ cups chicken broth
6 cups crusty whole wheat bread, cut into ½-inch cubes
1 cup tart dried cherries
Freshly ground black pepper

1. Bring the water to a boil in a 2-quart saucepan; add the rice and ½ teaspoon of the salt. Cover, reduce the heat to medium-low, and cook until the rice is tender and the grains have begun to split, about 40 minutes. Drain in a fine-mesh sieve. Preheat the oven to 325°F and butter a shallow 3-quart baking dish.
2. Heat the oil in a large sauté pan over medium-high heat, add the onion and celery, and cook until the onion is translucent, about 8 minutes. Add the apple, poultry seasoning, parsley, and remaining salt. Cook for 5 minutes. Add the broth and bring to a boil; remove from the heat.
3. In a large mixing bowl, combine the rice, apple mixture, bread, and cherries; season with salt and pepper. Spread the mixture evenly into the prepared baking dish and cover tightly with foil.
4. Bake until heated through, about 40 minutes. Remove the foil, bake for 10 minutes to crisp the top, and serve. To bake the stuffing in delicata squash: halve the squash lengthwise and scoop out seeds and stringy bits with a soupspoon. Season squash with salt and pepper, stuff, and bake, covered with foil, in a baking dish for 40 minutes, or until squash is tender when pierced with a paring knife. Uncover, bake 10 minutes to crisp top of stuffing, and serve.

Fresh Cranberry Chutney

8 servings

Fresh cranberries are available from fall through early winter. Their tart and fruity flavor combines well with the heat of chile, ginger, and Indian spices in this new take on cranberry sauce. I think you'll find it's drastically better than the tooth-achingly sweet canned cranberry jellies normally set out on the holiday table. Try it as a nice counterpoint to the richness of roast leg of lamb, duck, or Christmas goose.

1 tablespoon vegetable oil
½ cup finely chopped onion
1 tablespoon minced serrano chile
1 tablespoon minced ginger
12 ounces fresh cranberries
1 large pear, peeled, cored, and finely diced
⅔ cup sugar
1 pinch salt
Juice and zest of 1 orange
1 teaspoon garam masala*
1 cup finely chopped cilantro

1. In a medium saucepan, heat the oil over medium-high heat. Add the onion, chile, and ginger and sauté until the onion is translucent, about 8 minutes. Reduce the heat to medium and add the cranberries, pear, sugar, salt, and orange juice.
2. Bring the mixture to a simmer and cook, stirring occasionally, until all the cranberries have popped and the mixture resembles jam, about 30 minutes. Add a few tablespoons of water while simmering if the chutney begins to scorch on the bottom.
3. Remove the pan from the heat and stir in the orange zest, garam masala, and cilantro; allow to cool to room temperature before serving. The chutney is best when made one day ahead. Keep refrigerated in an airtight container for up to 1 week.

* Garam masala is an Indian spice mixture believed to be heating to the blood; in Hindi ***garam*** means "hot." It is available ready-made in some grocery and specialty stores, but I recommend you make your own for the best flavor. In a dry sauté pan, toast 15 teaspoons green cardamom pods, one 3-inch cinnamon stick, 1 teaspoon whole cloves, 1 tablespoon black peppercorns, 25 tablespoons cumin seeds, and 25 tablespoons coriander seeds over medium heat until fragrant. Grind the spices in a mortar and pestle or clean spice grinder to a fine powder. Refrigerate for up to 6 months.

Hazelnut Polenta Cake with Winter Fruit Compote

8 servings

Good-quality dried fruit is stewed with port and spices to accompany a not-too-sweet Italian polenta cake in this wintery recipe. Many fruit growers are drying their fruit and selling it at farmer's markets to extend the season. You'll be amazed at how good dried fruit can be when it's freshly made—it's much more moist and flavorful than the bulk dried fruit in grocery stores.

½ cup (1 stick) unsalted butter, at room temperature
1 cup sugar
2 large eggs
Zest and juice from 2 oranges
2 teaspoons vanilla extract
½ cup ricotta cheese
1 cup hazelnut meal, or 1½ cups hazelnuts ground to make 1 cup
½ cup polenta or coarse cornmeal
½ cup unbleached all-purpose flour
1 teaspoon baking powder
½ teaspoon salt
2½ cups Winter Fruit Compote (see recipe, page 212)

1. Preheat the oven to 375°F and lightly grease a 9-inch springform pan.
2. Beat the butter and sugar together in a large mixing bowl. Add the eggs one at a time, beating after each addition. Add the orange zest, vanilla, and ricotta, and beat to combine.
3. In a small dry sauté pan, gently toast the hazelnut meal, stirring constantly until it is lightly browned and smells delicious. Pour it into a medium bowl; add the polenta, flour, baking powder, and salt; whisk to combine.
4. Add half the hazelnut mixture to the egg mixture and beat briefly to combine. Add half of the orange juice and stir. Repeat with the remaining hazelnut mixture and juice. Do not overmix or the cake will be tough. Pour the batter into the prepared pan and bake until golden brown, about 35 minutes. Allow the cake to cool in the pan for 10 minutes, release the sides of the pan, and then serve warm with the fruit compote.

Winter Fruit Compote

2½ cups

¾ cup ruby port wine
½ cup water
¾ cup sugar
1 cinnamon stick
½ vanilla bean, split lengthwise
2 whole cloves
4 ounces dried apricots, diced
2 ounces dried cherries
2 ounces black currants
4 dried Mission figs, diced
1 fresh pear, peeled, cored, and diced

1. Combine the wine, water, sugar, cinnamon stick, vanilla bean, and cloves in a small saucepan and bring to a simmer over medium-high heat. Add the apricots, cherries, currants, figs, and pear; reduce the heat to maintain a gentle simmer. Cook until the fruit is tender, about 20 minutes.
2. Remove the cinnamon stick, vanilla bean, and cloves; partially drain the fruit and then serve with polenta cake. The compote can be made up to 2 weeks ahead without the pear and kept in an airtight container in the refrigerator. To reheat, combine the compote and diced pear in a small saucepan over medium heat until the pear is tender, about 20 minutes.

Lemon Semolina Cakes with Honey Thyme Frozen Yogurt and Citrus Fruit

8 servings

Beekeepers sell honey at almost all farmer's markets. They offer a wide range of flavors, from delicate orange to bold buckwheat, each honey reflecting the flowers from which the bees collected pollen. Experiment with the flavors to find honeys you like. Top-quality honey may be expensive, but consider that a bee must collect pollen from 2 million flowers to make one pound of honey!

Pastry Chef Michelle Vernier of Wildwood uses mild local honey to sweeten the frozen yogurt in this recipe, then she pairs it with moist pudding cakes and winter citrus fruit for a light, upscale dessert.

1½ cups Pastry Cream, still warm (see recipe, page 214)
1 teaspoon lemon zest
1½ tablespoons lemon juice
¼ cup semolina flour
¾ cup pastry flour
½ cup plus 6 tablespoons sugar, divided
¼ teaspoon salt
1½ teaspoons baking powder
4 egg whites*
1 pink grapefruit
1 seedless tangerine
1 Cara Cara or navel orange
1 blood orange
2 tablespoons orange blossom honey or honey of choice
1 tablespoon white rum (optional)
1½ quarts Honey Thyme Frozen Yogurt (see recipe, page 215)

1. Preheat the oven to 350°F and spray 2 cupcake tins with nonstick cooking spray.
2. In a large mixing bowl, combine the pastry cream with the lemon zest, lemon juice, and semolina flour. In a small bowl, sift the pastry flour, 6 tablespoons of the sugar, salt, and baking powder; stir into the pastry cream.
3. Whip the egg whites with an electric mixer until foamy. Slowly add the remaining sugar and continue to beat until stiff, glossy peaks form when the beaters are lifted. With a rubber spatula, gently fold the egg whites into the cake batter in 3 batches.

▸ *continued*

4. Divide the batter among the cupcake wells and gently smooth the tops with the back of a spoon. Bake until the cakes feel dry and a skewer inserted in the center of a cake comes out clean, 12 to 15 minutes. Do not overbake. Remove the tins from the oven and cool on a wire rack.
5. While the cakes are cooling, prepare the grapefruit, tangerine, and oranges. With a sharp paring knife, cut a slice off the top and bottom of each fruit. Using vertical cuts, trim away all rind and white pith. Hold each fruit over a small saucepan, slide the knife down one side of the clear membrane that divides the fruit into segments; repeat with the other side of the segment and place in a bowl. Repeat with the remaining segments.
6. Squeeze the membranes over the saucepan to extract any extra juice and discard them. Add the honey and any accumulated juice from the fruit bowl and bring to a simmer over medium-high heat; simmer until the mixture is slightly reduced, about 4 minutes. Stir in the rum and pour over the reserved fruit.
7. Put the cakes on dessert plates. Top with scoops of the frozen yogurt, spoon citrus fruit around them, and serve.

* You'll have 2 egg whites available from the pastry cream recipe.

Pastry Cream

1½ cups

⅓ cup whole milk

⅓ cup heavy cream

2 large egg yolks, whites reserved

2 tablespoons sugar

1 teaspoon all-purpose flour

4 teaspoons cornstarch

1 pinch salt

½ teaspoon vanilla extract

7 tablespoons unsalted butter, at room temperature

1. Heat the milk and cream over medium-low heat in a small, heavy-bottomed saucepan until bubbles appear around the edges.
2. Whisk the egg yolks, sugar, flour, cornstarch, and salt in a small bowl. Gradually whisk in the hot milk mixture, ½ cup at a time. Return the mixture to the saucepan and cook over medium-low heat, whisking constantly, until the mixture is a thick mayonnaise consistency. Do not boil or it will curdle. Remove from the heat, stir in the vanilla and butter, and whisk until the butter melts. The pastry cream can be made ahead and stored in an airtight container in the refrigerator for up to 4 days. Before using, bring cream to room temperature by letting it stand for 30 minutes.

Honey Thyme Frozen Yogurt

1½ quarts

½ cup heavy cream

1 tablespoon fresh thyme leaves, stems removed

¾ cup sugar

½ cup orange flower honey or other flavor

3½ cups low-fat yogurt

1. Cook the cream, thyme, and sugar in a small saucepan over low heat for 10 minutes. Remove from the heat and allow the mixture to steep for 10 minutes. Strain through a fine-mesh sieve into a medium bowl.
2. Whisk the honey and yogurt into the bowl and refrigerate until cold. Pour the mixture into an ice cream maker and freeze according to manufacturer's instructions.

Real Gingerbread Cake with Apple Cider Glaze

8 servings

Pastry Chef Melissa Lehmkuhl of ROUX uses fresh ginger to give this old-world cake a little kick. She frosts the cake with a sweet glaze of locally made apple cider and confectioners' sugar. Apple cider sold by the growers at farmer's markets tends to be made with better-quality fruit; in some states it is not pasteurized so it can retain its unique flavor.

3⅓ cups cake flour
2 teaspoons baking soda
1 teaspoon salt
½ teaspoon ground cloves
½ teaspoon ground nutmeg
¼ teaspoon ground mace
1 cup (2 sticks) unsalted butter, at room temperature
1¼ cups light brown sugar, firmly packed
4 large eggs, at room temperature
2 tablespoons finely minced ginger
½ cup molasses
1⅓ cups buttermilk
1 cup apple cider
2 cups confectioners' sugar, sifted
¼ cup crystallized ginger, finely chopped

1. Preheat the oven to 325°F. Lightly coat one 10-cup-capacity bundt pan or five 6- by 3-inch mini loaf pans with nonstick cooking spray.
2. Sift the flour, baking soda, salt, cloves, nutmeg, and mace in a medium bowl.
3. In a large mixing bowl, beat the butter and brown sugar together until fluffy and light. Add the eggs, one at a time, beating well after each addition. Add the ginger and molasses and mix well to incorporate.
4. In 3 batches, add the flour mixture to the butter mixture, alternating with the buttermilk, beginning and ending with the flour mixture.
5. Pour the batter into the prepared pan and bake until a wooden skewer inserted in the center comes out with moist crumbs clinging to it, about 1 hour and 15 minutes for the bundt pan, about 45 minutes for the mini loaf pans. Transfer to a wire rack and allow to cool for 1 hour.
6. Bring the apple cider to a boil in a small saucepan over medium-high heat; boil until reduced to about 3 tablespoons of thick syrup. Combine with the confectioners' sugar and whisk until smooth. Frost cake with the glaze, sprinkle with the crystallized ginger, and serve.

RESOURCES

A list of products referred to in this book.

CHEESES

Goat Cheese:

Alsea Acre Goat Cheese
888-316-4628
www.alseaacre.com

Fraga Farm
28580 Pleasant Valley Road
Sweet Home, OR 97386
541-367-3891
www.fragafarm.com

Rogue River Blue Cheese:

The Rogue Creamery
PO Box 3606
Central Point, OR 97502
866-396-4704
www.roguecreamery.com

DUNGENESS CRAB

Linda Brand Crab
http://marketnavigators.com

FRUIT

Hood River Fruit Loop Tour
www.hoodriverfruitloop.com

Cherries, Dried or Fresh:

Cherry Country
6200 Oak Grove Road
Rickreall, OR 97371
1-877-3CHERRY
www.thecherrycountry.com

GRAINS

Farro:

Bluebird Grain Farms
PO Box 1082
Winthrop, WA 98862
509-996-3526
www.bluebirdgrainfarms.com

Spelt and Other Whole Grains:

Bob's Red Mill
www.bobsredmill.com

HAZELNUTS, HAZELNUT MEAL, AND WILD RICE

Freddy Guys Hazelnuts
12145 Elkins Road
Monmouth, OR 97361
503-606-0458
www.freddyguys.com

KITCHENWARE

Canning Equipment:

Kitchen Krafts
www.kitchenkrafts.com
1-800-298-5389

Spaetzle Makers, Food Mills, Peelers, and Other Foodie Toys:

Sur La Table
www.surlatable.com

SPICES

Espelette Pepper and Fleur de Sel:

The Spanish Table
www.spanishtable.com

High Quality Bulk Spices:

Penzeys Spices
www.penzeys.com

TRUFFLES, TRUFFLE OIL, AND PORCINI MUSHROOMS

La Buona Tavola Truffle Cafe
1524 Pike Place
Seattle, WA 98101
206-292-5555
www.trufflecafe.com

THE CHEFS

The chefs mentioned in this book took time out of their hectic sixty-plus hour work weeks to contribute recipes to this book because they are so passionate about the *Farm to Table* message. Their passion and dedication to cooking market-driven food and maintaining close relationships with local farmers and purveyors is both inspiring and delicious. I urge you to patronize their restaurants and support their mission.

BLUEHOUR
Chef Kenny Giambalvo
250 NW 13th Avenue
Portland, OR 97209
503-226-3394
www.bluehouronline.com

BOAT STREET CAFE
Chef Renee Erickson
3131 Western Avenue
Seattle, WA 98121
206-632-4602
www.boatstreetcafe.com

CARAFE
Chef Pascal Sauton
200 SW Market Street
Portland, OR 97201
503-248-0004
www.carafebistro.com

CARMELITA
Chef Ande Janousek
7314 Greenwood Avenue N
Seattle, WA 98103
206-706-7703
www.carmelita.net

CELILO RESTAURANT AND BAR
Chef Ben Stenn
16 Oak Street
Hood River, OR 97031
541-386-5710
www.celilorestaurant.com

CRUSH
Chef Jason Wilson
2319 E. Madison Street
Seattle, WA 98112
206-302-7874
www.chefjasonwilson.com

LEENA EZEKIEL
Chef Instructor and Caterer
Portland, OR 97209
503-284-7796
leezekiel@aol.com

FIFE
Chef Marco Shaw
4440 NE Fremont Street
Portland, OR 97213
971-222-3433
www.fiferestaurant.com

THE FARM CAFÉ
Chef Fearn Smith
10 SE 7th Avenue
Portland, OR 97214
503-736-3276
www.thefarmcafe.net

LARK
Chef Johnathan Sundstrom
926 12th Avenue
Seattle, WA 98112
206-323-5275
www.larkseattle.com

PALEY'S PLACE
Chef Vitaly Paley
1204 NW 21st Avenue
Portland, OR 97209
503-243-2403
www.paleysplace.net

PARK KITCHEN
Chef Scott Dolich
422 NW 8th Street
Portland, OR 97209
503-223-7275
www.parkkitchen.com

PEARL BAKERY
Lee Posey
Tim Healea
102 NW 9th Avenue
Portland, OR 97209
503-827-0910
www.pearlbakery.com

ROUX
Pastry Chef Melissa Lehmkuhl
1700 N. Killingsworth Street
Portland, OR 97217
503-285-1200
www.rouxrestaurant.us

SIMPATICA CATERING AND DINING HALL
Chef Jason Owens
828 SE Ash Street
Portland, OR 97214
503-235-1600
www.simpaticacatering.com

TILTH
Chef Maria Hines
1411 N. 45th Street
Seattle, WA 98103
206-633-0801
www.tilthrestaurant.com

WILDWOOD
Executive Chef Dustin Clark
Pastry Chef Michelle Vernier
1221 NW 21st Avenue
Portland, OR 97209
503-248-9663
www.wildwoodrestaurant.com

FINDING MARKETS, CSAS, AND PRODUCTS NEAR YOU

ECOTRUST (www.ecotrust.org) is a Portland-based conservation organization committed to strengthening communities and the environment from Alaska to California. Ecotrust works with native peoples and the fishery, forestry, and food industries to build a regional economy based on social and ecological opportunities. Their "State of the Salmon" initiative closely monitors the health and welfare of Pacific salmon stocks.

EDIBLE COMMUNITIES (www.ediblecommunities.com) is a publishing and information services company that is devoted to connecting consumers to their food sources with regionally produced magazines, Web sites, and events. Find copies of edible community magazines at their Web site.

FOOD ROUTES (www.foodroutes.org/localfood) is a national non-profit organization that maintains online resources including an interactive "Buy Local" map that helps shoppers source farmers, markets, co-ops, restaurants, and CSAs by zip code.

LOCAL HARVEST (www.localharvest.org) is another site to help you find locally produced food in your area, including interactive learning materials.

MONTEREY BAY AQUARIUM SEAFOOD WATCH (www.mbayaq.org) is a program that provides information on how to be a responsible seafood consumer by buying fish from sustainable sources. The MBASW Web site provides a handy printable wallet-sized chart to remind you of which fish are a responsible choice and which are not.

SUSTAINABLE TABLE (www.sustainabletable.org) features a searchable database to help consumers find locally produced food, and includes recipes, videos, cookbook reviews, and blogs about all things local and delicious.

SEED SAVERS EXCHANGE (www.seedsavers.org) is a non-profit organization of passionate gardeners who save and share heirloom seeds to help maintain the world's vegetable and fruit diversity. It's an excellent source for information on various types of heirloom edibles with a lively discussion board.

BIBLIOGRAPHY

I consulted many books, articles, and reports during my research for this book. The following sources were particularly helpful.

"A Shoppers Guide to Pesticides in Produce," by R. Wiles, K. Davies, S. Elderkin. Washington: Environmental Working Group, 1996.

Barron's Food Lover's Companion, 3rd Edition, by Sharon Tyler Herbst. New York: Barron's Publishing.

Chez Panisse Vegetables, by Alice Waters. New York: HarperCollins Publishers, Inc, 1996.

"Globetrotting Food Will Travel Farther Than Ever This Thanksgiving," by Worldwatch Institute. Washington, DC: November 2002.

Fields of Plenty: A Farmer's Journey in Search of Real Food and the People Who Grow It, by Michael Ableman, California: Chronicle Books, 2005.

"Fruit and Vegetable Benefits," by National Centers for Disease Control and Prevention, Atlanta, GA: August 2006.

Plenty: One Man, One Woman, and a Raucous Year of Eating Locally, by Alisa Smith and JB Mackinnon. New York: Harmony Books (Random House), 2007.

Vegetables From Amaranth to Zucchini, by Elizabeth Schneider. New York: Morrow Publishing, 2001.

"What Are Burpless Cucumbers?" by Todd C. Wehner, HortiTechnology 10:317–320, Raleigh, NC: 2000.

INDEX

Page number in boldface indicates photograph

C

D

E

F

G

H

I

J

K

L

M

N

O

P

Q

R

S

T

V

W

Y

Z

ABOUT THE AUTHOR

IVY MANNING is a freelance food writer, cooking instructor, and personal chef. Her work has been featured in *Cooking Light*, *Fine Cooking*, *Best Places Northwest*, *Sunset*, *The Oregonian*, and on her Web site, www.chefivy.com. She lives with her husband and dog, Alice B. Toklas, in a house with a tiny kitchen in Portland, Oregon.